THE
HORSE
EQUESTRIAN
BUSINESS

Julie Brega

J.A. Allen
London

British Library Cataloguing in Publication Data
A catalogue record for this book is available
from the British Library

ISBN 0.85131.589.5

Published in Great Britain in 1994 by
J.A. Allen & Company Limited,
1, Lower Grosvenor Place,
Buckingham Palace Road,
London, SW1W OEL

Designed by Nancy Lawrence

Typeset in Hong Kong by Setrite Typesetters Ltd
Printed in Hong Kong by Dah Hua Printing Press Co.

(m) 636 . 668 B

THE
HORSE
EQUESTRIAN
—BUSINESS—

CONTENTS

LIST OF
ILLUSTRATIONS

LIST OF TABLES

ACKNOWLEDGEMENTS

I would like to thank the following friends for their invaluable help in the production of this book:

Debby Baker, for typesetting the original manuscript.

Kitty Best, for all illustrations.

Bob Emery, for hours spent calculating the financial tables, forecasts and budgets.

Also my father, John Hollywood, for advice on the first-aid section and, finally, special thanks to my husband, Bill, for his constant help and support.

INTRODUCTION

The Horse: Equestrian Business is one of six books in the Progressive Series. This series forms the basis of an advanced open learning course offered by The Open College of Equestrian Studies. The information contained in these books, particularly in this book, is equivalent to, or exceeds that required by the British Horse Society's Stage IV qualification.

The main objective of these books is to present the information needed by the equestrian enthusiast, whether professional or non-professional, in a clear and logical manner.

Business skills must be considered of equal importance to equestrian skills when running a commercial enterprise, as many equestrian businesses fail through lack of planning expertise. At the outset, careful planning is essential — market research should be carried out to establish the viability of the business idea. This is fully discussed, including the process of discovering what personal qualities, as well as business ones, are necessary. The next step is to prepare the business plan, cash flow forecast and profit and loss budget. The method of calculating these figures, and examples of the cash flow forecast and profit and loss budget are given.

Once the business is established, an efficient and straightforward system of recording payments and receipts must be set up. A step-by-step guide to simple bookkeeping is presented, with examples from the cash book and other documentation.

Other financial matters covered include taxation and VAT accounting.

When planning or running a business, the legal implications must be considered. The law of contract and its relevance to the equestrian business is dealt with, as is the law of tort, under which fall civil wrongs such as negligence and trespass. Within the section entitled 'Employing People', contracts of employment, dismissal and working pupil arrangements are discussed. The Health and Safety at Work Act 1974 is relevant to all employers, so health and safety guidelines relating to equestrian businesses are highlighted.

It is essential that any person involved with horses receives adequate first aid training. The section on accident procedure describes the action to be taken after a simple or serious fall; how to deal with an unconscious casualty, including resuscitation techniques and the recovery position, and how to recognize and immobilize fractures before the casualty is taken to hospital.

The section on staff management covers topics such as the principles of yard organization, the skills needed by the yard manager, and training programmes. Public relations and advertising conclude the book.

1

PLANNING AN EQUESTRIAN BUSINESS

The equestrian industry covers a wide spectrum of horse-related activities, the majority of which are enjoying expansion as more people turn to the horse in their pursuit of pleasure. Running an equestrian business can be a rewarding challenge — it can also be a nightmare of financial and administrative problems dotted throughout an organizational minefield!

Many equestrian businesses operate for love of the horse, but this on its own is not enough — for a business to survive it must at worst break even, but should ideally make a profit.

Good planning will improve any business's chances of survival. Many skills other than equestrian ones are needed when in business with horses. This is true whether running one's own yard or acting as yard manager for an employer. In this book these various additional skills are discussed, ranging from the initial planning of the new enterprise through the administration of all financial and legal aspects and on to the way in which the people of the business are managed.

INITIAL PLANNING

Having decided to set up a business, plans must be drawn up. Research shows that approximately 85 per cent of businesses fail within the first five years. Horse-related businesses have a tendency to change hands frequently and often fail due to a lack of initial planning.

Problems facing the equestrian business include:

1) Getting established.

2) Consolidating the business once established.

3) Coping with expansion.

4) Limited financial resources.

5) Labour-intensive nature of horses.

6) Very high costs associated with keeping horses.

7) Seasonality — unless an indoor school is available, earnings drop in the winter months. In the case of a hunting and/or point-to-point yard, the summer months will prove quiet.

The equestrian business manager might lack skills in the following areas:

1) Financial planning and record keeping.

2) Staff management and training.

3) Marketing.

4) Public relations.

5) The law and insurance.

Specialists may have to be consulted in these areas.

Good plans are fundamental to both survival and long term profitability. These plans include market research, the business plan, cash flow forecast and profit and loss budget.

MARKET RESEARCH

Market research is the starting point in establishing the viability of any business idea and is simply to do with 'finding out' — it need not be an expensive process. The process involves discovering the answers to the following questions:

Do you possess the necessary personal qualities to make the business a success?

What services will you offer?

What are the goals and objectives of the business?

Who will be your clients?

Why will they be your clients?

Where will your clients come from?

Who are your competitors?

What premises will you use? Can you acquire planning permission?

What will be the scale of the business?

What form will the business take?

Will you need to employ staff?

What are the principal risks faced by the business?

What can be done to minimize these risks?

Let us examine these matters in more detail.

Requisite personal qualities

Running your own business requires certain personal qualities. Deciding whether you possess them requires a degree of self-analysis. The requisite personal qualities include:

Motivation.

A positive attitude.

Energy.

Initiative.

Self-confidence.

Determination.

Persistence.

A realistic approach.

Good judgement.

Self discipline.

Mental and physical good health.

Questions which need to be asked and answered include whether you can:

Work harder?

Work for longer hours?

Forego perks such as holidays?

Solve problems?

Think up new ideas and make them work?

Handle several different things at the same time without getting confused?

Get on well with people (even awkward ones)?

Accept expert advice?

Do you know your subject and market thoroughly?

Family support is essential: will your family encourage and support you? Are they happy to be involved and take the risks associated with running your own business? Is there any member of the family, particularly the spouse, who is against the idea?

Services on offer

The broader the range of services offered, the larger the potential clientele will be. Some businesses specialize in specific aspects of equestrianism whilst others provide an all-round service. Services offered may include a combination of the following:

Livery. Full, working, grass or DIY.

Exercise and schooling. May be part of a full livery arrangement.

Breaking and training. Only to be undertaken by skilled staff.

Instruction. Group and private lessons, novices ranging from toddlers and nervous mums through to inexperienced men. More experienced riders will require instruction to a higher level. Riding for the disabled is a most important aspect.

Trekking/hacking. Good countryside with minimal roadwork is desirable.

Hire of horses/ponies. For hunting, shows, Pony/Riding Club rallies etc.

Competition training. For horse and rider combinations.

Exam training. In preparation for professional qualifications. (Will accommodation be needed?)

Stable management instruction. Courses of various lengths, lectures, demonstrations etc.

Dealing. Buying and selling.

Clipping and trimming.

Hiring out facilities. Manège, indoor school, showjumps and cross-country course.

Specialist Spheres. Examples include:
   Driving, polo, showing etc.
   Lecture/demonstrations by renowned competition riders.
   Horse transportation.
   Breeding. Stud facilities may include stallion services, mares taken for foaling etc.
   Racing. Breaking and training.
   Competitions.
   Tack shop. This may also sell horse/pet feedstuff.
   Rehabilitation and therapeutic facilities.

The goals and objectives of the business

At the outset, the objectives of the business should be defined, and ways of achieving them planned. The business idea will need to be well thought out to ensure that you are providing the right service in the right place, at the right time, for the right price.

THE RIGHT WAY AHEAD

Offer   **THE RIGHT SERVICE** ⟶ High quality livery, instruction, training etc.

           IN THE RIGHT PLACE ⟶ Ideally, location should suit yard, (near centre of population with good riding countryside).

           AT THE RIGHT TIME ⟶ When there is a demand, supply the service (e.g. hunter liveries).

           FOR THE RIGHT PRICE ⟶ This does not mean cheap! Properly calculated fees are essential.

Prospective clients

The clientele envisaged will affect the nature of your advertising campaign. Your clients will fall into at least some of the following categories:

Professionals within the equestrian industry.

Non-professional.

Male/female — young/old?

Total beginner; novice; fairly competent.

Competitive/non-competitive.

Very keen/fairly keen/not that keen but want to 'have a go'.

There are many reasons why people ride horses:

To improve professional qualifications.

To achieve competitive goals.

To take part in long-distance rides.

For relaxation.

To improve fitness.

For fun and enjoyment.

For the sense of achievement.

To overcome fear and nervousness, and to gain confidence.

To be with horses.

To meet people.

To enjoy the countryside.

To go hunting.

To enhance social status.

Riding can be enjoyed by disabled and able-bodied people alike.

Why people will be your clients

In any line of business, the chief reason why people become and, importantly, remain clients is quality of service. Offer a high quality in every aspect of the business including:

1) The way in which the telephone is answered. Whoever answers the phone should be polite, cheerful and helpful.

2) The way in which a visitor is greeted on the yard. All members of staff must be taught to offer assistance politely and to identify any persons found on the yard.

3) The atmosphere and appearance of the premises. The staff should be well turned out, polite and friendly. The yard, office and stables should be exceptionally clean and tidy at all times.

4) The standard of horsecare and stable management. The horses must look and feel well, be neatly turned out in clean, well fitting tack.

5) Instruction and training. Well qualified staff should be motivated into giving their highest standard of teaching to all clients whether it is their first lesson of the day or their last; this is a very good reason for not overworking instructors or horses. Students and working pupils on the yard must be trained thoroughly and not treated as cheap labour.

6) Customer care and general efficiency. This must cover every level and every aspect of yard management. Quality breeds success — people will associate the business with quality and will want to remain among the clientele.

Where your clients will come from
This will depend upon various factors:

1) Whether your yard is near large towns and villages.

2) Establishments offering specialist training (for example from a top competition trainer) will attract clients from further afield.

3) The better the facilities, the further people will travel.

4) It may be necessary to offer accommodation in order to encourage people to travel long distances.

5) Once your reputation as a high class business is established people will be happy to travel to reach you.

Who your competitors are

It is almost certain that you will face some sort of competition. Research along the following lines will be necessary:

1) Where are they based? Will people travel to you even though your competitor is nearer to them? How are you going to encourage them to come to you? .

2) Find out if a similar business to yours is proposing to set up in the same area. You may find out by asking the planning

department in the local council offices.

3) If a local competitor has recently closed down, try to find out why.

4) Obtain any informative literature offered by your competitor or visit their yard and find out what services they offer and how much they charge.

Premises to be used: can you acquire planning permission?

Very often the family home and existing land and buildings is to be used for business purposes. Less frequently a prospective entrepreneur sets out to buy a premises specifically with a view to running a business from there.

Before purchasing a property, it is essential to investigate the council's likely reaction to your application to run an equestrian business from there — the solicitor should be instructed to undertake this task.

Planning permission is needed for any development involving change of use, even though no structural alterations or additions may be required. Therefore a private residential property or farm must have approval from the planning authorities to be used for riding school or similar activities. The exception to this is that, if erecting a building of $30\,m^2$ or smaller, planning permission is not needed.

An architect or chartered surveyor can help with planning matters, although their services are expensive. An architect will investigate a potential business premises, obtain planning permission, estimate costs, draw up plans, prepare contracts and supervise building work to completion. Architects also advise on structural alterations and fire and health and safety regulations. Surveyors can advise on the structural condition of premises and the planning requirements for the adaptation of existing buildings.

Should planning permission be refused the applicant has the right to appeal. Ultimately the appeal could be made to the Secretary of State for the Environment and this may involve a public enquiry. When considering a planning application the authorities take into account:

1) The suitability of the site.

2) The provision of any development plans and restrictions in that locality.

3) The impact on amenities and the character of the area.

4) Changes in the volume and type of traffic, access and road safety.

5) Aesthetic appearance of buildings and materials used.

6) Drainage — the effects of any extra burden on mains water and sewerage.

7) The possibility of job creation (most areas are keen to reduce their unemployment figures).

8) The effects on the landscape and wildlife.

9) Noise, pollution and any other associated nuisances.

All building works are subject to building regulations. The architect will obtain the relevant forms and organize meetings and approval with the local building control officer.

When considering the purchase of premises further points need to be taken into account:

1) Location — this should be suitable for the nature of the business, for example, a trekking centre will need vast areas of countryside while a racing yard will need gallops and relatively good access to racecourses.

2) Access — the better the motorway and main road links, the easier it is for clients to reach the business.

3) Centres of population — riding schools in particular need to be situated close to large towns in order to provide the necessary volume of clients.

4) Reputation — if buying an existing business, find out whether it has a good or bad reputation. This helps you to plan your business idea and marketing strategy.

The scale of the business

To a certain extent this is dependent upon:

1) The size of the premises and the amount of land available if using existing land and buildings.

2) Any restrictions imposed, for example by planning authorities.

3) The number of staff employed.

4) Services offered.

5) The number and variety of types of horses and ponies kept for instruction purposes.

The form the business will take

This should be discussed with experts such as the accountant, bank manager and solicitor. There are three basic forms of small business:

Sole trader

Advantages. This is a simple and flexible form of business which can be set up immediately with few formalities. The Inland Revenue must be informed — income tax payable is based on net profits.

Disadvantages. The owner of the business is totally liable for all losses. In some circumstances two classes of National Insurance Contributions may have to be paid but some social security benefits may be lost.

Partnership

Advantages. The workload and responsibilities are shared.

Disadvantages. Partners are 'jointly and severally' liable for all of the partnership's debts. Each partner is liable for the whole amount of debts incurred by another, even if they knew nothing about the debt. Also, the business owner loses sole control and all profits are shared.

Before going into partnership it is important to ask, 'Do I need a partner?', 'Will profits double as a result of having a partner?, 'Do the advantages outweigh the disadvantages?' Before proceeding, a partnership agreement should be drawn up and legal advice sought before finalizing it.

Limited companies

Advantages. The company has its own identity, distinct from that of its directors. The directors are not personally liable for any debts incurred by the company.

Disadvantages. The start-up process is quite complicated and there are many restrictions and formalities. It is essential to discuss company formation with a solicitor.

The need to employ staff

If so:

How many?

What tasks will they perform?

What qualifications and skills will they need?

What training will they need?

Who will provide this training?

Will it be in-house or elsewhere?

Where will you find them?

What will you pay them?

Will there be other perks, for example keep of horse, food and accommodation?

Have you budgeted for this?

The principal risks faced by the business

Equestrian businesses are exposed to many risks which, without sufficient attention to minimization, can cause the downfall of the enterprise. These risks include:

1) High overheads, such as mortgage/rent on equestrian property, rates on buildings and so on.

2) Very high costs of keeping horses.

3) Loss of use of animals for reasons such as lameness or the outbreak of an infectious or contagious ailment.

4) Seasonal variances — most establishments have a busy season when income is high, but during the closed season income is greatly reduced. For example a riding school without an indoor school or all-weather surface will suffer a great loss of earnings during the winter.

Minimizing the risks

1) Try to reduce overheads wherever possible.

2) Try to minimize the costs of keeping horses without making false economies. For example look for good quality feed and hay at competitive prices and try to negotiate a discount. Buying hay and straw directly off the field is much cheaper than buying barn-stored hay.

3) Try to prevent illness and lameness. Do not overwork riding school mounts. Keep shoeing, teeth rasping, worming and inoculations up to date.

4) Try to budget for any slack periods and think of means of earning money during these times. For example the bad weather may cause lessons to be cancelled, so advertise your mobile clipping service or run a stable management course.

5) Depending upon your type of business, look into the cost-effectiveness of building an indoor school. By the time you have considered all costs of purchase, rates and so on, you have to run a very large and busy establishment to make it worthwhile. It may be more realistic to investigate outdoor all-weather manèges.

PREPARING THE BUSINESS PLAN

The business plan helps to ensure that the business has the potential to be profitable — a point that will be very important in any bank manager's opinion whenever considering the loan of money. It also ensures that the business owner fully understands the extent of all financial commitments and that he has researched his market to help maximize the business potential. Any problems may be identified early and dealt with before they affect the business.

The rough draft

Decide on the structure of the plan — work out what headings you require and in what order. The business plan is a lengthy and important document so care and time need to go into its preparation. Acquire all information and figures before trying to write it. Most banks can provide pre-prepared business plan forms as part of their Small Business Advice Packs. The business plan should be: realistic, workable, clear, well presented and properly documented.

Once you are happy with the handwritten plan, type it up and take copies. Present it in a neat document file or ring binder along with the projected profit and loss budget and cash flow forecast. If you have arranged to visit the bank, the business plan and other figures should be presented to the manager a few days in advance, thus providing the opportunity to read it before your meeting.

The structure

A number of headings are required. A suggested format includes the following:

Synopsis. An introductory page which can be read in a short space of time, outlining the key points of the business plan.

Introduction. Give the business name and details of any logo to be used. State what form the business is to take; whether sole trader, partnership or limited company. Introduce the business with a general outline of what you intend to do and how the business will develop.

Personal details. Give your full name, address, date of birth and details of professional qualifications. Describe briefly what previous experience you have had and why you wish to run your own business. Lenders are always happier dealing with people with a good track record. Never be dishonest about any of your previous financial failures or mistakes — the banks have ways of finding out before they lend you their money.

Services. Explain the nature of all services you will offer.

The Market. Give accurate details of the market (customers — who, where and why).

Marketing. Calculate the cost of your marketing campaign. Give information about where and when you will advertise.

Premises, Horses, Equipment. What is available, what you will need and how much they will cost.

Personnel. The staff you will need, their qualifications and/or experience and what you will pay them.

Record (Bookkeeping) System. How you intend keeping the books. Details of which bookkeeper (if any) and accountant you will use.

Objectives. Outline the objectives for the different areas of the business and describe what you want out of the business and over what period of time, both short term (up to one year) and medium term (one to five years). You could also try to provide an outline prediction of the long term future of the business.

Finance. Give details of all assets, their value and life expectancy. The bank will be interested in your collateral, i.e. what security you can pledge as a guarantee for repayment of the money. It is essential that you can provide some form of security if you wish to borrow money.

Prepare a list of costs — how often these costs are incurred and when they have to be paid for. Also, produce and attach:

1) Cash flow forecast.

2) A projected trading and profit and loss budget.

These should cover the first twelve months of business. Always include realistic living expenses.

Explain how you arrived at these figures and how you anticipate the business will develop financially, bearing in mind that initially income is low and outgoings are high. A simple break-down of these figures should be prepared. The advice of the accountant may be sought to help with preparation of financial forecasts.

Other information should include the name of the business's solicitor. Also state whether the business is VAT registered or not and mention insurance policies and any other relevant information. The question of whether the business should be registered for VAT is an important one which you should discuss with your accountant. This topic is dealt with fully further on (Indirect Taxes and VAT Accounting)

PREPARING FINANCIAL FORECASTS

All financial forecasts have to be based to a certain extent on assumptions — reasonable guesses based on knowledge, experience and current information. The following have to be estimated:

1) Value of all assets.

2) Depreciation of assets.

3) Direct costs (purchases or cost of sales).

4) Indirect costs (overheads).

Once these figures have been calculated, the fees to be charged for the various services on offer can be worked out. It would be sensible to check these fees with those charged by any other local business competitor. It is then possible to estimate:

1) The value of sales, i.e. income.

2) If relevant, the VAT paid to the business and by the business.

Costs to be calculated

Assets
These include items such as:
Premises (including indoor school and outdoor manège).

Cross-country course.	Showjumps.
Machinery.	Vehicles.
Paddock fencing.	Field shelter.
Wooden sectional stables.	Yard equipment.
Fire-fighting equipment.	Horses and ponies.
Tack and equipment.	Office furniture.

Depreciation
All assets except for land and property should be depreciated by between 10 and 25 per cent per year depending upon how long you expect them to last.

Direct costs
The main ones are:
Feed, hay, straw and other bedding materials.
Shoeing.
Veterinary fees.
Groom's wages.

Indirect costs

Salaries/wages (administrative staff).	Riding school licence.
Mortgage/rent/rates/water.	Council tax.
Insurance.	Interest charges.
Repairs/renewals.	Advertising.
Heat/light/power.	
Printing/stationery/postage.	
Transport/petrol/road tax.	
Telephone.	
Professional fees (solicitor, accountant, etc.)	

Preparing the cash flow forecast

The purposes of the cash flow forecast are:

1) To show when and how much money is expected to come in.

2) To show when and how much money is planned to go out.

This will identify any cash surplus or deficit, thus allowing you to plan either a deposit account for the surplus or an overdraft facility to accommodate the deficit.

The process of preparing the cash flow forecast is as follows:

1) Estimate sales, exclusive of VAT, bearing in mind factors such as seasonal variations and the time it takes to build up business.

2) Calculate the VAT on these sales (if you are to be VAT registered).

3) Record capital introduced, bank loans and any other large sums of money other than those earned through sales.

4) Estimate what payments will be made, exclusive of VAT, and when. List them in the appropriate column. *Note that non-cash items such as depreciation do not appear on the cash flow forecast.*

5) Total payments up and record them in the subtotals column.

6) Estimate the cost of assets you need to purchase, and place in the appropriate column.

7) Record VAT on payments in the next row (if you are to be VAT registered).

8) Estimate drawings (the amount of money you will take out of the business for your own use).

9) At the end of each three months, calculate the total VAT on sales and deduct the VAT on purchases. The net figure is payable to or receivable from HM Customs and Excise in the following month and should be entered accordingly.

10) Finally, the total payments figure is calculated and deducted from the total receipts figure to give the net cash flow in or out. This should be added to or deducted from the opening balance to give the closing bank balance.

11) The closing bank balance for January will be the opening bank balance for February and so on. (See Table 1).

By following the calculations in Table 1 through it can be seen that this imaginary business will have a net cash inflow of £3,054 in the first year of business.

When calculating a cash flow forecast your assumptions must always be realistic: over-optimistic expectations will not give you or your bank manager a true idea of the business.

The sample cash flow for the imaginary equestrian business shows high outgoings and low income initially. The closing bank balances shown indicate the level of overdraft facility or similar which is going to be needed in order to get this business going.

The bank manager will also want reassurance that this business will start to make a profit after the first year. In the case of an equestrian business it would be sensible to make a forecast for the second year of business when the income will (hopefully) have increased.

Ways of improving cash flow

1) Invoice promptly and encourage prompt payment. Obviously it is desirable to encourage your clients to pay their outstanding debts with a friendly telephone call before resorting to the solicitor, but do not allow bad debts to drag on. Most firms of solicitors offer a debt-collecting scheme whereby they charge a small percentage of the total value of the debt once it is successfully recouped.

2) Pay takings into the bank regularly to keep the overdraft to a minimum. Any surplus cash should be transferred to a deposit account to earn interest. Keep just enough in the current account to cover outgoings.

Table 1. Cash Flow Forecast. 12 Months to 31st December 199X

	Jan.	Feb.	March	April	May
A OPENING BALANCE	Nil	(5612)	(6632)	(8638)	(11137)
RECEIPTS					
Cash Sales (Ex. VAT)	360	520	720	800	1200
Credit Sales (Ex. VAT)					
Output VAT (on Sales)	63	91	126	140	210
Capital Introduced	4000				
Bank Loan	10000				
B TOTAL RECEIPTS	14423	611	846	940	1410
PAYMENTS (EX. VAT)					
Feed/Bedding	250	250	600	600	600
Vet/Farrier Fees *	—	250	250	275	275
Wages inc. Tax/N. Insurance	500	500	900	900	900
Rent/Rates	937	—	—	938	—
Insurance	166	167	166	167	167
Repairs *	500	200	100	100	50
Advertising *	—	—	110	—	—
Printing/Stationery *	50	—	—	50	—
Transport *	20	30	40	60	70
Telephone *	10	—	—	90	—
Professional Fees *	—	—	100	—	—
Interest Charges	—	—	375	—	—
Subtotal	2433	1397	2266	3180	2062
Assets Purchased +	17000	—	—	—	—
Input VAT (on Purchases)	452	84	86	101	69
Drawings	150	150	500	500	500
VAT Payments/(Repayments)	—	—	—	(342)	—
C TOTAL PAYMENTS	20035	1631	2852	3439	2631
D NET FLOW IN/(OUT) B – C	(5612)	(1020)	(2006)	(2499)	(1221)
E CLOSING BALANCE A – D	(5612)	(6632)	(8638)	(11137)	(12350)

Note: All figures shown in brackets are negative.
* It has been assumed that VAT at standard rate (currently 17.5%) is payable on these items, except for Assets+ where it has been applied to equipment only.

June	July	Aug.	Sept.	Oct.	Nov.	Dec.	TOTAL
(12358)	(13027)	(13929)	(9831)	(3806)	(52)	3388	Nil
1800	3000	5800	7000	8000	4700	2775	36675
	200	200	600	600	800	500	2900
315	560	1050	1330	1505	962	573	6925
							4000
							10000
2115	3760	7050	8930	10105	6462	3848	60500
600	600	700	700	700	700	700	7000
275	275	275	275	275	275	275	2975
900	900	900	900	900	900	900	10000
—	937	—	—	938	—	—	3750
167	—	—	—	—	—	—	1000
50	500	200	100	100	50	50	2000
110	110	—	110	—	110	—	550
—	—	50	—	—	—	50	200
90	120	200	200	200	200	120	1350
—	120	—	—	120	—	—	340
—	—	—	—	—	150	—	250
375	—	—	375	—	—	375	1500
2192	3562	2325	2285	3233	2385	2095	29415
—	—	—	—	—	—	—	17000
92	197	127	120	122	137	87	1674
500	500	500	500	500	500	500	5300
—	403	—	—	2496	—	—	2557
2784	4662	2952	2905	6351	3022	2682	55946
(669)	(902)	4098	6025	3754	3440	1166	4179
(13027)	(13929)	(9831)	(3806)	(52)	2263	4554	3054

3) Pay large fixed bills, such as insurance premiums, by instalments.

4) Constantly renegotiate credit and discount terms with suppliers.

5) Budget for large items, such as the hay you wish to purchase off the field in May. In the months leading up to this try to save a certain amount regularly so you have enough to pay for the hay. Also try to arrange with the farmer to pay in two or more smaller sums rather than one lump sum.

Over-optimistic expectations will not give you or your bank manager a true idea of the business — better to err slightly on the side of caution!

Preparing the trading and profit and loss budget

The purposes of the trading and profit and loss budget are to show the estimated net profit or loss of the business before tax and to show how much you estimate the business will cost to run on a monthly basis.

The figures to be used are the same as in your cash flow forecast, but modified as follows:

1) Credit sales must be entered when they are made, *not* when the cash is collected — this can be one or two months later.

2) Similarly, expenses must be entered when they are incurred, *not* when they are paid. Again they can be paid one or more months later.

3) Break your costs down between direct costs and overheads.

4) Do not include capital items, bank loan or assets purchased.

5) Depreciation on your assets must be calculated and included.

A trading and profit and loss account is shown in Table 2, using the same figures (adjusted as explained above) as those for the cash flow forecast in Table 1.

As can be seen, this imaginary new riding school will make a profit of £6,950 in the first year of business and over the same period generate a cash inflow of £3,054. These would be satisfactory after the first year's trading. To complete the figures that the bank would want to see, a balance sheet should also be prepared. In a functioning business, this would be part of the annual accounts. For further information see annual accounts (page 39) and Table 7 (page 40).

Alternative forecasts could also be prepared to see how the business would stand if sales figures were increased or decreased. This would show you whether the business could survive on lower sales, and it could be developed to see what your 'break even' point is — that is, the minimum income to keep the business 'ticking over'.

Once the business plan, cash flow forecast and trading and profit and loss budget have been completed the business owner can answer the following questions:

1) Do I need to borrow money?

2) If so, how much?

3) When?

4) How am I going to pay it back?

5) What security can I offer?

6) How much can I afford to repay each month?

When seeking a bank loan or similar it is vital that *expert advice* is sought from the bank manager, accountant or small business adviser.

Armed with the answers to the above questions, get quotes from different reliable sources and find out:

1) What is the cost of borrowing money?

2) When and how will the cost be paid?

3) Over what period will the repayments be made?

4) What will be the *total* expenditure?

5) What *extra* charges might be involved?

**Table 2. Trading and Profit and Loss Account: Budget Example —
12 Months to 31st December 199X**

	Jan.	Feb.	March	April	May
SALES	360	520	720	800	1200
Less –DIRECT COSTS					
Feed and Bedding	250	250	600	600	600
Vet/Farrier Fees	250	250	275	275	275
Wages (Groom)	250	250	450	450	450
TOTAL	750	750	1325	1325	1325
GROSS PROFIT/(LOSS)	(390)	(230)	(605)	(525)	(125)
OVERHEADS					
Wages (Office)	250	250	450	450	450
Rent/Rates	312	313	312	313	312
Insurance	83	83	84	83	83
Repairs	500	200	100	100	50
Advertising			110		
Printing/Stationery	50			50	
Transport	20	30	40	60	70
Telephone	25	25	40	40	40
Professional Fees		100			
Interest Charges	125	125	125	125	125
Depreciation	187	188	187	188	187
TOTAL	1552	1314	1448	1409	1317
NET PROFIT/(LOSS) BEFORE					
DRAWINGS AND TAX	(1942)	(1544)	(2053)	(1934)	(1442)

June	July	Aug.	Sept.	Oct.	Nov.	Dec.	TOTAL
2000	3200	6400	7600	8800	5200	3200	40000
600	600	600	600	600	600	600	6500
275	275	275	275	275	275	275	3250
450	450	450	450	450	450	450	5000
1325	1325	1325	1325	1325	1325	1325	14750
675	1875	5075	6275	7475	3875	1875	25250
450	450	450	450	450	450	450	5000
313	312	313	312	313	312	313	3750
84	83	83	84	83	83	84	1000
50	500	200	100	100	50	50	2000
110	110		110		110		550
		50				50	200
90	120	200	200	200	200	120	1350
40	40	40	40	40	40	40	450
				150			250
125	125	125	125	125	125	125	1500
188	187	188	187	188	187	188	2250
1450	1927	1649	1608	1649	1557	1420	18300
(775)	(52)	3426	4667	5826	2318	455	6950

FINANCIAL MANAGEMENT

The majority of equestrian business proprietors have a deep knowledge of equestrian matters and are dedicated to their work, putting in very long hours in often unfavourable conditions. Hard though they may work, however, there are many who take only a little (if any) interest in the financial aspects of the business, so many equestrian businesses fail or fall into dire financial straits due to poor business planning and money management. There is often the assumption that, because the riding school has large cash takings on a Saturday, 'everything must be all right'. This, combined with a 'head in the sand' attitude, invariably leads to problems.

Financial matters tend to be left to the bookkeeper and accountant because, apart from a lack of knowledge, the equestrian business proprietor does not have the time to spend doing all of the bookwork. It is, of course, an excellent idea to pay a skilled bookkeeper and accountant as the proprietor is then free, allowing him or her to create income through teaching, breaking, schooling etc. However, a basic understanding of the principles of bookkeeping and business planning may well lead to more efficient organization of money matters which in turn will improve the chances of making a profit. Thus, when running any sort of equestrian business, one should aim, as far as practicable, to be a business manager as well as a yard manager and/or instructor.

Record keeping

There are numerous books written on the subjects of bookkeeping and financial management. Most colleges offer evening classes and there are various Open Learning (home study) courses available for those who wish to acquire a good knowledge of these subjects.

While it is beyond the scope of this book to discuss these specialist subjects fully, there are certain matters which any equestrian business manager needs to understand in principle. Therefore, the main aims of this section of the book are:

1) To familiarize the student with the terms and expressions used when discussing financial matters.

2) To offer a broad outline explanation of the topics to help remove any shroud of mystery.

3) To offer a basic insight into these 'broad outlines' so that when discussing financial matters with the bookkeeper or accountant the concepts may be more easily understood.

Why keep records?

There is a statutory requirement to keep adequate records in order that the Inland Revenue can correctly assess your profits for tax purposes. Also, good financial records need to be kept in order to answer the following questions:

What is the value of fixed and current assets?

What are the overheads?

What are the variable costs?

How much does the business owe?

How much is owed to the business?

What profit is the business making?

What is the current cash position of the business?

Is it necessary to register for VAT?

The final set of accounts as submitted to the Inland Revenue is used as the basis for the assessment of income tax payable. Ideally, however, one should not have to wait for the annual accounts before being able to answer these questions. Effective financial control ensures that:

The overall performance of the business is constantly and closely monitored.

Cash flow is managed effectively.

Problems can be spotted in advance and action taken.

The process of accounting may be divided into two parts:

1) The development and keeping of accurate and full records of all financial activities of the business.

2) The interpretation of these records.

Records which need to be kept

The records kept depend to a certain extent upon the nature of the business, but main requirements are:

'Dawn of Day One' Records. These are the figures recorded on day one of the business's first financial year. Your accountant will call these your opening balances.

Cash Records. Records of daily receipts and payments made by cash or cheque must be kept, in order to calculate profit and loss. A petty cash book should be kept for small, low value purchases.

Bank Account Records. All banking transactions must be checked through the regular preparation of bank reconciliation statements.

VAT Records. If the business is registered with HM Customs and Excise, VAT records must be kept.

Wages Records. These must be kept when staff are employed.

The start of business

Records have to be maintained from the first moment of the first day of business, i.e. 'dawn of day one'.

An opening balance sheet must be drawn up showing all assets and liabilities. These figures are then carried forward to the appropriate columns in the records books and are recorded as if they happened on day one of week one, even though they were arranged in the weeks leading up to the start of business. In preparation for the start of business one must:

1) Decide which bookkeeping system to use.

2) Decide whether to register for VAT and do so before day one. The criteria for deciding whether or not to register for VAT are referred to later in this book (Indirect Taxes).

3) Have a filing system ready for the efficient storage of invoices.

How to keep records

When deciding how to keep the records it is important to consider simplicity and usefulness. Complicated systems deter most busy people from attempting to keep the bookwork up to date.

The system chosen must be useful to the particular type of business without being excessively time-consuming. There are many bookkeeping systems to choose from — most fit into one of the following categories:

1) Analysed cash book or single entry method.

2) Off-the-shelf systems.

3) Double entry method.

4) Computerized systems.

Analysed cash book

This is the simplest method and also forms the basis for the proprietary off-the-shelf systems.

A large bound cash book can be bought to provide an effective but straightforward method of recording all cash received and payments made. Such books are available already ruled into a number of columns on each page and the columns can be headed to suit your particular requirements. The columns on the left are used to record receipts and those on the right to record payments.

Examples of cash book pages are shown in Tables 3 and 5. The following is a brief description of how to operate a simple analysed cash book. The references will be to entries in Table 3 — Receipts and Table 5 — Payments.

Table 3. Cash Book: Receipts

Date	Details	Bank	Cheque	
1.10.92	Daily Receipts Diary		126.90	
2.10.92	Daily Receipts Diary		94.00	
2.10.92	County Plus Insurance Co.	574.40	330.00	
3.10.92	Daily Receipts Diary		47.00	
4.10.92	Daily Receipts Diary	211.50	129.25	
5.10.92	Daily Receipts Diary		58.75	
6.10.92	Daily Receipts Diary	176.25	94.00	
30.10.92	Daily Receipts Diary	82.25	82.25	
	TOTAL	1044.40	962.15	
		A	B	

$A = B + C = D + E + F$

Recording receipts

All receipts (or takings) must be recorded in the cash book. Details should include:

Date payment was received.

The total amount of the transaction.

A description of the service, for example a lesson, hack, livery account. (When taking money for lessons, payments should also be recorded by the client's name in the bookings diary.)

How much VAT is included (only if you are VAT registered).

Whether payment was by cheque or cash.

Receipts which are not for ordinary takings are entered into a column headed 'other receipts' and a short explanation is given in the details column.

Cash	VAT	'Ordinary' Lessons, Livery etc.	Amount	Other Description
23.50	22.40	128.00		
–.–	14.00	80.00		
–.–			330.00	Insurance Claim
11.75	8.75	50.00		
23.50	22.75	130.00		
23.50	12.25	70.00		
–.–	14.00	80.00		
–.–	12.25	70.00		
82.25	106.40	608.00	330.00	
C	D	E	F	

As each page is used, the totals in each column should be calculated and taken forward to the following pages until the end of the month when the totals should be ruled off.

At the end of each day the till or cash box should be emptied and the contents counted to ensure that it tallies with the record of receipts. The normal float, used for giving change, can then be returned to the cash box. Details of gross daily takings for both cash and credit customers are entered in the daily receipts diary (see Table 4) and the total entered into the receipts side of the cash book.

For treatment of VAT, see VAT Accounting.

Sales invoices

As well as cash or cheque takings you will need to prepare sales invoices for customers for whom you have opened an account. These invoices can be for tuition, liveries and so on. The following simple procedures should be adhered to:

Table 4. Example Page of Daily Receipts Diary

Date: 1.10.92					
Name	Details	Type	Cash Customers	Credit Customers	
		Cash/ Chq.	Amount	Inv. No.	Amount
Mr A. Smith	Private lesson	Cash	11.75		
Mrs Wilson	Private lesson	Chq.	11.75		
Mr Pickard	September A/c.	Chq.		12001	70.50
Mrs Jones	September A/c.	Chq.		12004	35.25
Mrs Lewis	1 hr. Group lesson	Cash	11.75		
Holly Edmunds	Group lesson (Jnr.)	Chq.	9.40		
	Total		44.65		105.75
	VAT		6.65		15.75
	Goods		38.00		90.00
			44.65		105.75

Cash	23.50
Cheques	126.90
	150.40

1) Agree terms on which the account will be operated. For example, an invoice will be rendered for all services at the end of each month, which is payable within seven days.

2) Prepare all invoices promptly and include all details of charges together with the date on which payment is due.

3) Keep a copy in a file for 'unpaid invoices'.

4) When the cheque is received, take the invoice out of the unpaid file: enter the date on which payment was received together with the cheque number.

5) Record in the daily receipts diary.

6) Pay into bank together with any other cheque or cash takings.

7) Transfer paid invoice into a 'paid invoices' file.

If VAT registered, certain information must be shown on the invoice (See VAT Accounting).

Paying money into the Bank

It is not safe to keep large sums of money on the premises — and the money is better employed in the bank account keeping the overdraft down or earning interest and ensuring that there are sufficient funds to cover payments made by the business. Takings must therefore be banked promptly.

A record of the names and addresses of clients who have paid by cheque should be kept, as cheques can go astray in the course of clearing. Ideally, cheques to the value of £50.00 or less should be validated with the drawer's bank card number which guarantees that the cheque will be honoured.

The slip in the paying-in book must be carefully filled in, giving all cheque names and amounts. Be sure to use the carbon paper and have a copy of the slip. This should be attached to the appropriate daily receipts diary(ies) and filed. When cash and cheques are paid into the bank the total is entered into the 'bank' column. This must agree with the paying-in slip and all the entries made under cash receipts since the previous time money was paid into the bank.

Table 5. Cash Book: Payments

Date	Details	Ref:	Total	VAT	Wages
1.10.92	Mr Brown	10001	117.50	17.50	
2.10.92	Office Supplies UK	Cash	58.75	8.75	
3.10.92	British Telecom	10002	84.60	12.60	
3.10.92	Wages – Jane	10003	50.00		50.00
3.10.92	Wages – Betty	10004	50.00		50.00
4.10.92	Tax and N. Insurance	10005	12.50		12.50
4.10.92	Self	10006	75.00		
5.10.92	Greens Feed Merchant	10007	70.50		
6.10.92	Northwest Trailer Co.	10008	235.00	35.00	
30.10.92	Mr White O/S	10015	105.75	15.75	
30.10.92	Bank Charges	D/D	3.50		
	TOTAL		863.10	89.60	112.50
			A	B	C

$$A - B = C + D + E + F + G + H + I + J$$

Recording payments

Only record in the cash book when a payment is actually made. Wherever possible pay by cheque or credit card, not by cash. If you have to pay by cash, try to do so only for small amounts through petty cash (see page 37) and always obtain a properly receipted invoice.

There will be several columns required to analyse the types of payments you will be making (see Table 5); careful attention to the number of columns and what they will be used for will be time well spent. Most of your payments will be for items of revenue expenditure such as bedding, feed, veterinary and farriery charges. Since your capital payments (for buying assets) will be infrequent, you will only need two columns for them — one for the amount and one to describe the type of asset

Feed, Hay, Bedding	Vet, Farrier	Telephone	Stationery Office Supplies	Drawings	Other	Capital Amount	Details
	100.00						
			50.00				
		72.00					
				75.00			
70.50							
						200.00	Small trailer
	90.00						
					3.50		
70.50	190.00	72.00	50.00	75.00	3.50	200.00	

D	E	F	G	H	I	J

purchased.

Payments should only be made after the goods or services have been received and against a properly prepared invoice from your supplier. Invoices should be numbered and stored in a date order file on the date upon which they must be paid. If for any reason the invoice has to be stored elsewhere, keep a copy or written description in the file on the appropriate date.

On the due date, write out the cheque, detach the remittance advice slip from the invoice (if one is provided) and send it with the cheque to the creditor. Record the payment accordingly: write on the invoice the date it was paid and the cheque number before transferring it to a file for paid invoices. If you are paying wages, the amounts paid and all amounts for tax and National Insurance should be entered into a wages column.

As with receipts, as each page is used the totals in each column should be calculated and taken forward to the following page until the end of the month, when the totals for payments and receipts should both be ruled off on the same page.

Value added tax

If you are registered for VAT you must have a separate column for VAT for both receipts and payments. The figures entered into your analysis columns must then *exclude* VAT (see VAT Accounting). If, however, you are not registered for VAT then the VAT columns are not necessary and your analysis must be done *including* VAT.

Bank reconciliation

At the end of each month you must calculate the balance in your cash book. Before doing this you must refer to your bank statement, which you should request monthly, and enter into the payments side of your cash book all the standing orders and direct debit payments which have been made by your bank during the month. If you receive any fees by standing order these should similarly be entered into the cash receipts side. Make sure that you check the bank's details very carefully — they can make mistakes.

You will then be able to calculate your cash book balance, which is done by taking your balance at the end of the previous month, adding all receipts and then deducting all payments in respect of the current month. This must then be compared and reconciled to the balance on the bank statement at the end of the month. The balances will rarely be the same. This can be due to:

1) Cheques made out to a supplier and entered in the cash book but not yet presented for payment by the supplier (unpresented cheques).

2) Cheques and/or cash paid into the bank and entered in the cash book but not yet credited to your account (cheques/cash in transit).

3) Mistakes — they can be made!

You must then compare entries in your cash book and the bank statement. Tick off from the bank statement every item that appears on both: the entries now left in your cash book are those that the bank has not yet recorded.

Each type of entry should be added up. The total of type 1) above is deducted from, and type 2) added to, the balance per the bank statement. The final figure (assuming there were no errors!) should be equal to the cash book balance. If it is not, check carefully for errors. If there are any queries or problems, contact your bank. A bank reconciliation would look like this:

Table 6. Bank Reconciliation – October 1992 (Based on figures in Tables 3 and 5)

Cash book opening balance		Nil
Cash receipts		1044.40
Cash payments		863.10
	Closing balance	<u>181.30</u>
Balance per bank statement		204.80
Deduct –	Unpresented cheques 10015 Mr. White	105.75
Add –	Cash/Cheques in transit 30.10.92	82.75
	Balance per cash book	<u>181.30</u>

Once the reconciliation has been prepared and agreed it should be filed away as proof that the bank statement has been thoroughly checked and that the cash book is correct.

The petty cash book

Every business should have a petty cash book and box. Within the box there should be a small book of petty cash vouchers. At the beginning of the week the amount of money in the box is noted in the petty cash book by the petty cashier. The jobs of the petty cashier are:

1) The control of petty cash.

2) To make payments when appropriate and to keep records of payments made.

3) To balance the petty cash book at regular intervals.

Low value payments which would clutter up the cash book are recorded in the petty cash book. These may include items such as tea, coffee, biscuits etc. Payments should only be made against the correct documentation, that is, a petty cash voucher signed by the petty cashier. Receipts should be attached to the relevant petty cash voucher. The petty cash should be replenished by drawing cash from the bank to restore it to its original amount.

Other bookkeeping systems

Off-the-shelf systems
There are several off-the-shelf proprietary systems such as Simplex or Kalamazoo which take some of the repetitive work out of the analysed cash book. Your bookkeeper or accountant may be able to recommend a suitable one.

Double entry method
This is more complex and requires setting up and maintaining a manual double entry bookkeeping system. It is only really necessary when your business becomes very large and even under these circumstances a better alternative would be to use a computer system.

Computer systems
Whatever the size or nature of the business, every bookkeeping procedure can be computerized. There is a huge range of accounting software systems available, making the task of keeping records simpler and quicker. A computer software dealer will offer advice on suitable systems — there are systems specially designed for the specific requirements of equestrian businesses.

It is possible to purchase a computer, visual display unit, keyboard and printer for under £1,000.00 and this would certainly represent a good investment for the business with a lot of data to record. The chief advantage of using a computerized bookkeeping system is that the piece of data is only keyed into the computer once. The computer then does everything with the figure that needs to be done. This greatly reduces the amount of time spent updating records. Some systems go right through to preparing the final accounts and will ask for any missing figures needed. These final accounts can be asked for every day if required — all at the push of a single key.

Thus, time and effort can be saved provided the proprietor and staff have the knowledge needed to operate the computer. Computer skills may be acquired by attending evening classes at technical college, moreover, the software dealer will guide the computer operator initially and most companies offer an after-sales advice service.

Stocktaking

At the end of the financial year, in order to prepare annual accounts, the value of all unsold stock is ascertained. All items, including horses for sale are accounted for. Two figures are needed: the cost price, and the figure it is hoped to realize upon sale. Each item is valued at the lower price and is recorded as closing stock. This figure is carried over onto the next financial year where it becomes opening stock.

Annual accounts

These are prepared by the accountant at the end of each financial year, and should be compared to the original budget. Consideration should also be given to doing this on a monthly or quarterly basis for businesses during the start-up phase. This may also be required by the bank as a condition of providing a loan or overdraft facility. The annual accounts consist of:

1) The trading and profit and loss account. An example of this has been given in Table 2 where the TOTAL columns only would be prepared.

2) The balance sheet which is a list of the business's assets and liabilities at the end of the year. An example of a

balance sheet based on our imaginary business is shown in Table 7.

Table 7. Balance Sheet as at 31st December 199X

			£
Fixed Assets:			
Cost –	Buildings		10,000
	Equipment		2,000
	Motor car		5,000
			17,000
Less –	Depreciation		2,250
	Net Fixed Assets		14,750
Financed by Long Term Loan			10,000
			4,750
Current Assets:	Stock (feed, bedding)	500	
	Debtors (inc. VAT)	500	
	Cash	3,054	4,054
Current Liabilities:	Creditors (inc. VAT)	452	
	VAT	2,702	3,154
	Net Current Assets		900
			5,650
Represented by:			
	Capital		4,000
	Profit for year	6,950	
	Less drawings	5,300	1,650
			5,650

Once the annual accounts are completed and agreed, your accountant will agree with the Inland Revenue the amount of tax to be paid, and will then submit a bill to the business. Accountants are expensive, so the business owner must ensure that all the financial records are complete and in order. This will make it quicker and easier for these accounts to be drawn up and thus less expensive.

GLOSSARY OF TERMS

This glossary is provided to clarify the meanings of unfamiliar terms used when discussing financial matters.

Accruals. These are services/goods used but not yet paid for and are shown on the balance sheet as current liabilities.

Annual Accounts. The recorded summary of all financial aspects of the business, prepared by the accountant and presented to the Inland Revenue.

Assets. Items owned by the business that have a measurable money value. They are divided into:

1) Fixed assets — premises, equipment, vehicles etc. that are retained for a long time and are not generally for re-sale.

2) Current assets — short term assets that will not last longer than one year, for example stock, outstanding debtors, cash and prepayments (items/services paid for but not yet received).

Audit. A process carried out by an independent accountant (an auditor) on a company's annual accounts. (Not carried out on a sole trader's accounts.)

Balance Sheet. A statement of a business's assets and liabilities.

Business Plan. An analysis of the nature of the business and a forecast of expected business activities.

Capital. Money contributed to the business by the owner and therefore owed by the business to the owner. This may be described as:

1) Total value of assets less total external liabilities, (money owed to banks, building societies and other creditors) or

2) Owner's investment plus net profit less drawings.

Capital Employed (working capital). Current assets less current liabilities. Used to keep the business working and to pay off creditors.

Capital Expenditure. Money used to buy fixed assets.

Cash Book. Daily record of payments and receipts whether made by cash or cheque.

Cash Flow. The process of total cash coming in and going out of the business over a period of time.

Cash Purchases. Purchases of goods paid for immediately by cheque or cash.

Cash Sales. Sales paid for immediately either by cash or cheque.

Cost of Sales. Term used in the trading account to represent cost of materials or items used which, when taken from your sales figure, gives you the gross profit.

Credit. The supply of goods or services without immediate payment.

Credit Purchases. Purchases paid for within agreed time limit.

Credit Sales. Sales to customers which should be paid for within time specified on the invoice.

Credit Account. Account held by a trusted customer.

Creditor. A supplier to whom the business owes money.

Debtor. A client who owes money to the business.

Depreciation. Method of measuring the cost of using an asset which decreases in value due to fair wear and tear.

Direct Costs. Expenses such as materials which vary according to services offered/sales achieved.

Drawings. Amounts of money or goods taken out of the business by the owner for his or her own use.

Facility. A loan or overdraft provided by a bank to a business.

Fiscal Year. The Inland Revenue operates on fiscal years from 6th April one year to 5th April of the next.

Financial Year. The accounting year of the business; twelve month period shown in the profit and loss account.

Fixed Cost. See overheads.

Gross Profit. Gross profit equals sales figure (turnover) less purchases figure (direct costs), found on the trading account. It is the profit made before the deduction of overheads.

Indirect Costs. See overheads.

Liabilities. Debts or future commitments of the business. Long-term liabilities include capital, bank loan/mortgage, that is the means of purchasing the assets. Headed as 'financed by' in the balance sheet. Current liabilities are those debts to be paid within twelve months, for example creditors, overdraft and accruals, i.e. services used but not yet invoiced for.

Liquid Asset. Asset which can be converted into cash very easily.

Net Profit. Net profit equals gross profit less expenses (overheads), found on the profit and loss account.

Overdraft. Extension of credit by bank on a current account.

Overheads. Expenses of the business. Most remain fixed regardless of turnover, for example rent, and may also be described as fixed or indirect costs. However, some, for example, staff costs, will vary according to business activity.

Petty Cash Book. The book used for recording all low value purchases bought with money from the petty cash box and recorded on the petty cash vouchers.

Profit and Loss Account. A statement showing sales, purchases, expenses and profits (or losses) for an accounting period, normally one year.

Purchases. Items bought with the intention of reselling in some form in the course of business.

Revenue Expenditure. Money spent on purchases.

Statement of Account. Received from bank or from a supplier, shows all relevant financial transactions and finishes with amount you owe or are owed.

Stock. Goods used in some form for resale. In a dealer's yard, horses; in a tack shop, tack.

Trading Account. Summary of sales and purchases for any period, usually one year, showing gross profits.

Turnover. The total sales for the year.

Variable Costs. See direct costs.

TAXATION

When in business it is desirable to have a knowledge of the broader implications of the different forms of taxes. Although it is beyond the scope of this book to deal with the full complexities of taxation, the basic principles will be discussed.

At the early planning stage of setting up the business a good accountant is needed. He or she will give professional advice on many financial aspects including:

1) The best bookkeeping system to use.

2) What form the business should take — sole trader, company etc.

3) The accounting date, that is the date by which the final accounts are drawn up each year.

4) Notifying the Inland Revenue of the date you intend to commence trading. The Inland Revenue is the government department responsible for the collection of most taxes, except for import duties and VAT, which are administered by HM Customs and Excise. Read the Inland Revenue's booklet *Starting in Business*. This contains the initial form required by the Inspector of Taxes.

There are three main categories of tax:

1) *Direct Taxes*:

Income Tax.
i) Pay As You Earn (PAYE) — for employees.
ii) Schedule D — for self-employed, either sole traders or partners.

Corporation Tax — payable by companies.

National Insurance — deductions from earnings used to finance pensions, sick pay and other benefits.

2) *Capital Taxes*:

Capital Gains Tax — tax on profits obtained from sale of a fixed asset.

Inheritance Tax — tax on capital transferred at death or within seven years before death.

3) *Indirect Taxes*:

VAT — tax payable on turnover exceeding the specified threshold. Businesses may become VAT registered voluntarily regardless of turnover.

Stamp Duty — tax payable by the purchaser of a property exceeding a value specified by the Chancellor of the Exchequer.

Customs and Excise Duties — on items such as petrol and alcohol.

Direct taxes

Income tax
This is collected in two ways:

1) *Pay as You Earn (PAYE).* The employer has to obtain income tax and National Insurance contributions from his staff on behalf of the government. Employees pay Schedule E income tax on the PAYE system. The relevant forms may be obtained from the local Inspector of Taxes. It may be necessary to ask your accountant to explain the PAYE documentation.

   Calculating PAYE is a very tedious and time-consuming procedure, but one which must be kept up to date from the first week of business. Tax is calculated on weekly or monthly earnings, taking into account any personal allowances. The accountant must advise in this respect.

2) *Schedule D.* Self-employed persons, whether sole traders or partners, receive a tax assessment in the autumn of every year based upon profit figures from the annual profit and loss account ending in the previous fiscal year. The Inland Revenue operates on fiscal years ending 5th April each year. For example, the fiscal year 1992/1993 runs from 6th April 1992 to 5th April 1993.

   The basic principle behind taxation of profits is that the net profit (the figure remaining after direct costs and overheads have been deducted from sales revenue), is the income of the proprietor or is shared between proprietors if there are two or more partners.

   The accounts for a set twelve month period are prepared and finalized by the accounting date, then submitted by your accountant to the tax office, usually with a letter explaining any points which might need clarification. The Inspector of Taxes may respond with a query or two. It is advisable to reply promptly to any queries — it may be necessary to visit the tax office.

Once the tax office agrees the figure representing profit, an assessment is made and sent to you. If you are not in agreement with this assessment an appeal must be made within thirty days. If the assessment is accepted, payment is generally made in two equal instalments on 1st January and 1st July, one year in arrears. This results in the self-employed person paying tax some fifteen months or so after starting up in business.

Corporation tax

When a limited company is formed, the directors draw a salary and are taxed on this salary as employees (i.e. PAYE). The company's accounts are drawn up and checked (audited) by an independent accountant to ensure that everything is in order. Wages/salaries are classed as a cost to the business.

When the accounts are finalized they are submitted to the Inland Revenue who then return an assessment — a percentage of the company's profits is taken as corporation tax, payable on 1st January in a single lump sum. All company accounts are then filed at Companies House. As the business is taxed as a separate entity it is important that the directors and accountant endeavour to minimize the amount of corporation tax paid.

National insurance

These contributions are deducted from earnings to pay for pensions, sick pay and other benefits. Advice regarding National Insurance is given by the Social Security office. There are four classes of contribution:

Class 1 is deducted from the wages of employees.

Class 2 is paid by self-employed people either by stamping a card or by direct debit via the bank.

Class 3 covers voluntary contributions.

Class 4 covers further contributions which may have to be made by a self-employed person. Such contributions are calculated on profits — the accountant's advice should be sought.

Capital taxes

Capital Gains Tax is a tax imposed on profits resulting from the sale of a fixed asset such as land or buildings.

Inheritance Tax. Any capital, for example property and/or an existing business, transferred upon death or within seven years before death, is subject to inheritance tax.

Indirect taxes: VAT

Stamp Duty and Customs and Excise Duties are not normally primary concerns of small businesses which do not import or export, so we will concentrate upon Value Added Tax (VAT). This tax is payable on goods and services supplied by businesses registered with the Customs and Excise office.

Businesses *must* be registered for VAT if the annual turnover exceeds the VAT threshold as set periodically by the Chancellor of the Exchequer. Businesses whose turnover does not exceed the threshold *may register voluntarily*. Voluntary registration may be undertaken by any business whether exceeding the VAT threshold or not.

The main advantage of registeration is that VAT may be claimed back on business purchases made. The chief disadvantage of being VAT registered is the increase in price to the client. This will make a business less competitive than a local, unregistered business. The paperwork involved can be laborious if records are not kept carefully up to date — your accountant will advise on VAT accounting.

Many leaflets explaining VAT, and the forms necessary for registration, are available from the Customs and Excise offices. Your accountant will be able to explain fully the 'ins and outs' of VAT.

If you register you will be given a number which is to be shown on all relevant paperwork including invoices, receipts and headed paper. Penalties for non- or late registration for VAT are severe. A business whose turnover has exceeded the threshold may well have to pay the appropriate VAT even though the clients have not been charged at VAT inclusive rates.

There are two rates of VAT — standard rate, which at the time of writing is 17.5 per cent, and zero rate.

When registered for VAT, the business charges tax to clients on taxable supplies and services. This is known as output tax. The business may claim back any VAT charged to it by others. This is known as input tax. If registered, you will be able to claim this back on purchases which relate to the business. These may include office equipment, the telephone bill and payments for business services, such as accountants, solicitors, farrier, vet. However, depending upon the legislation in force, there are items for which the VAT may not be claimed back. These currently include cars and supplies for business entertainments.

When selling zero-rated goods or services no VAT is charged, but the business is still able to reclaim input tax.

Some items and services are exempt from VAT, as is land. If selling exempt supplies, the business may not be able to claim back VAT. The VAT office issues leaflets detailing goods that are zero-rated or exempt and offers advice on claiming back input tax.

VAT rules are often different from Inland Revenue rules regarding deductions of taxes.

VAT accounting

This is a major accounting function of small businesses, and it is essential to understand the basics. There are financial penalties for failing to keep VAT records, therefore it is imperative that you keep all proof of inputs and outputs, i.e. tax invoices from suppliers and copies of tax invoices issued by yourself. Indeed, a record of all taxable goods and services supplied or received as part of the business must be kept, including both standard and zero-rated items. A separate record must be kept of all exempt supplies.

Tax invoices

No VAT may be claimed without a correctly made out tax invoice issued by a registered person. A tax invoice is a document showing certain information about what is being supplied. It should be issued within thirty days of the date the goods or services were supplied. The tax invoice must show:

1) An identifying number.

2) The name, address and registration number of the supplier.

3) The time of supply.

4) The customer's name and address.

5) Type/nature of the supply.

6) A description identifying the goods. Each description should include:
   (i)   Quantity/extent of supply.
   (ii) Charge made excluding VAT.
   (iii) Rate of VAT.

7) Total charge made excluding VAT.

8) Rate of any discount.

9) Total VAT payable.

For sales worth £50.00 or less including VAT, made direct to the public, a less detailed tax invoice may be issued showing only:

1) Supplier's name, address and VAT registration number.

2) Time of supply.

3) Description which identifies the goods supplied.

4) Charge made inclusive of VAT.

5) The rate of VAT.

If an invoice is paid by cash as opposed to cheque the supplier must, if asked, show on the invoice that payment has been received and the date of receipt.

The 'time of supply' is known as the 'tax point'. This is the date on which the supply of the goods or services is treated as taking place. VAT is charged at the rate in force at the tax point.

Calculating VAT — handy formulae
Assuming VAT is at 17.5 per cent:

When calculating amount of VAT in VAT inclusive cost:
   VAT inclusive cost $\div 47 \times 7$ = amount of VAT included.

When calculating how much VAT to add on to VAT exclusive cost:
   VAT exclusive cost $\times .175$ = amount of VAT of add.

Recording sales
This involves:

1) Issuing tax invoices for all standard rated sales unless using one of the retailing schemes. The retailing schemes allow you to keep records based on 'reconciliation of daily takings' figures. Invoices do not have to be issued unless a customer asks for one. HM Customs and Excise publish leaflets giving full information on the retailers' schemes. Riding school takings would be recorded under one of the schemes.

2) Issuing invoices which show the same information as tax invoices for any zero-rated or exempt sales made.

3) Keeping copies of all invoices and doing a summary of them.

   The sales summary involves numbering the invoice copies and recording the same numbers against the entries in the summary. Keep the numbers/invoices in order. Show separate totals for:

1) VAT on sales.

2) Sales exclusive of VAT.

3) Exempt sales.

4) VAT due on certain postal imports. (Seek advice if importing.)

5) Any credits allowed to clients.

At the end of each tax period, add up the VAT shown in these records and transfer it to the VAT account as output tax.

Recording purchases

All of the necessary details will be shown on the suppliers' tax invoices. Make a summary of them, numbering and listing them in order. Show separate totals for:

1) VAT you have been charged on purchases.

2) Values of purchases exclusive of VAT.

3) VAT on imports.

4) Credit from suppliers.

The length of credit you allow your clients or that suppliers allow you will affect the amount of VAT to be paid or reclaimed in each tax period. At the end of each tax period add up the total VAT paid on taxable purchases and transfer it onto the VAT account as input tax. Keep separate records of any business purchases on which you cannot deduct input tax, such as cars and business entertainment expenses.

VAT returns

Put simply, a VAT account is a summary of the totals of output and input tax for each tax period. A VAT period is normally quarterly. You can agree your quarter dates with your local VAT office. Keep an up-to-date record of the totals outlined and enter them into the VAT account with separate headings:

VAT deductible (input tax)	**VAT payable** (output tax)
Purchases	Sales
Imports	Certain postal imports
Errors in earlier returns	Errors in earlier returns
Any bad debt relief	

Take into account credits received or allowed and adjust accordingly. At the end of each tax period, subtract the input tax from the output tax and record the difference.

Use the figures from the VAT account to fill in the return. A leaflet is issued by the Customs and Excise office entitled *Filling in Your VAT Return.*

The VAT return and payment must be sent no later than one month after the end of the tax period. If by chance the input figure is greater than the output you can claim the difference back from Customs and Excise.

VAT registered organizations with a low turnover (currently under £350,000) may elect to account for VAT on a 'cash basis' which means you only account for VAT in each quarter in respect of sales invoices paid less purchase invoices paid. This is done by keeping VAT records in the cash book as shown in Tables 3 and 5. Since most riding stables will fall into this category, consideration should be given to electing to do this. However, your accountant should always be consulted.

Keeping VAT records

All registered businesses must kept the following records for a minimum of six years:

Orders and delivery notes.

Relevant business correspondence.

Purchase and sales books.

Cash books and other accounting books.

Purchase invoices and copy sales invoices.

Records of daily takings.

Annual accounts including profit and loss accounts.

Import and export documents.

Bank statements and paying-in slips.

VAT accounts.

Credit/debit notes issued or received.

Occasionally a VAT officer will arrange to visit the business premises and go through all records, so it is important that they are all kept safely and up to date. Any discrepancies will be noted and fully investigated.

As with all accounting matters the advice of a reputable accountant should be sought with matters relating to VAT. Alternatively, contact the VAT office and seek advice there.

VAT and horse sales

Up-to-date information on the complexities of VAT on horse sales in Great Britain can be obtained from the British Equestrian Trade Federation, Wothersome Grange, Bramham, Nr. Wetherby, Yorkshire, England LS23 6LY. VAT registered equestrian businesses who are involved in horse sales would be well advised to consult this body.

2

THE LAW AND ITS EFFECTS UPON THE BUSINESS – AN OUTLINE

When planning and/or running a business, the legal implications must be borne in mind.

This chapter deals with general aspects of laws which may have an impact on an equestrian business. More specific requirements relating to insurance and employing staff are discussed in Chapters 3 and 4 respectively.

Law is a vast, complex and ever-changing subject. Failure to understand your legal obligations can have important and expensive consequences, therefore at least a basic knowledge of the relevant law is needed so that the owner of a business will have some idea of when professional legal advice should be sought. While this section of the book offers a basic outline, it should be stressed that advice on a specific topic should always be sought from a solicitor.

However, when seeking legal advice, you should be as clear as you can in your own mind about the areas in which you need help. Ask for advice from friends or other professionals you deal with. Try to ask someone who knows what they are talking about — don't expect the person who dealt with your friend's divorce to be able to help with a problem involving breach of business contract.

When you think you have located the best source of assistance, phone up or see if you can arrange a free 'without obligation' interview. Explain your problem briefly and clearly and ask the professional to explain how he or she would be able to help you. Ask how the charges are made up and how big they are likely to be. If you have a financial ceiling, make this clear.

THE LAW IN ENGLAND AND WALES

Bear in mind that the law outside England and Wales may differ from that set out here.

One division of the law in England and Wales is that between statute and case law.

Statute laws are those passed by Parliament in the form of Acts and their associated regulations ('statutory instruments'). The influence of the European Community has increased enormously over the past few years — the Commission makes certain regulations that are directly applicable in member states, and directives to member states to alter their legislation to bring them into line with the directive.

Common or case law consists of an ever-increasing system of rules and principles laid down by the courts over the years as a result of judicial precedent. This is the system whereby a judge's decision in court is influenced by the decisions made by superior judges in previous, similar cases.

Another division of the law in England and Wales is that between criminal and civil, or private, law. However, one action may be both a breach of the criminal law and civil law.

Criminal law is concerned with offences against the public which are punishable by fine or imprisonment.

Civil law covers all aspects of action between citizens which is enforced by litigation in a private action in the High or County Court or perhaps some form of tribunal. Settlements may be in the form of monetary compensation (damages) or the imposition of injunctions (a court order to do, or not to do, something). Civil law is further divided into several areas including the law of contract and the law of tort. The former deals with legally binding agreements between people while the latter is concerned with civil wrongs such as negligence.

THE LAW OF CONTRACT

A contract is a legally binding agreement between two or more parties which may be made verbally or in writing. A verbal contract is usually as valid and enforceable as a written one; the only problem with a verbal contract is proving what its terms are.

When running an equestrian business the most common contracts are those relating to the sale of goods. Goods may include such things as horses, vehicles, tack, equipment, hay and straw.

Most sales made in the course of business are covered by the Sale of Goods Act 1979. A contract for the sale of goods is defined as one under which 'the seller transfers or agrees to transfer the property in goods to the buyer for a money consideration known as the price'.

Terms

Contracts consist of 'terms' — the details of the actual deal struck between buyer and seller. Terms may come from more than one source and may be both written and verbal. Terms dealing with the sale of goods commonly cover the following aspects:

1) The subject matter of the contract (what goods are being sold).

2) The price, when it will be paid and sometimes the seller's rights if it is not paid on time.

3) When ownership will pass (transfer of goods).

4) Promises the seller makes about the quality of the goods (warranties and conditions).

   In addition to those terms specifically agreed between both sides, or set out in 'standard terms of trading' some may be implied by statute. Sales made in the course of business have certain terms implied by the Sale of Goods Act 1979. These include:

5) That the goods will be of merchantable quality.

6) That the goods will be fit for their purpose.

7) That the goods will conform with any sample.

8) That the seller has the right to sell the goods.

It is worth looking at these terms in more detail:

1) *The subject matter of the contract.* It is important to identify exactly what is being sold.

2) *The price.* This is the payment agreed by both seller and buyer to be exchanged for the goods. If no price is agreed the Sale of Goods Act states that a reasonable price will be paid.

3) *The transfer of goods.* The transfer of ownership is not necessarily dependent upon payment of the price. The Sale of Goods Act 1979 says it passes when the goods are delivered unless both sides agree that ownership will pass at some other time.

   Some contracts specify (in a 'retention of title' clause) that ownership of goods will only pass on payment for them, so although the buyer might get physical possession of the goods he or she will not *own* them until they are paid for.

   Obviously, it is a good idea to incorporate a retention of

title clause in the contract when selling valuable goods, to enable you to repossess the goods if the buyer does not pay or becomes insolvent. It is important that the clause is actually part of the contract; the other side must know of its existence before the deal is struck. You cannot spring express contractual clauses on the other side after a deal has been done, let alone when things go wrong. It is for this reason that retention of title clauses on invoices are not only usually unenforceable, but worse than useless as they give a false sense of comfort.

A retention of title clause should incorporate ancillary rights (such as the right to enter premises to repossess goods). With some retention of title clauses you must also be able to identify exactly the goods that are not paid for. For example, if you were to supply 200 bales of hay under two contracts and you were still owed for 100 bales of hay and you wanted to repossess that 100, you would have to prove not only that they were *your* bales of hay but also that they were the bales unpaid for as opposed to the bales paid for.

Generally, the drafting of a workable retention of title clause needs an expert who will also explain to you (in advance) what to do if you have to exercise it. Enforcing a retention of title clause usually requires swift, positive action and so it is a good idea for you to know your rights and the best practical way of dealing with this beforehand.

'Sale or return' contracts will also vary the implied term about when ownership passes. Ownership in these circumstances is transferred when the buyer indicates an approval of the goods and intention to go ahead with the transaction. If no time limit is specified for acceptance of goods on sale or return, the buyer must act within a 'reasonable time'. What is 'reasonable' depends on the individual circumstances surrounding the particular contract.

4) *Warranties and conditions.* These are terms of the contract and, in contracts relating to the sale of goods, often relate to the quality of goods being sold. The distinction between warranties and conditions is a technical legal one and is not

within the scope of this book — if a warranty is broken the law makes available different legal remedies from when a condition is broken.

Warranties may be implied by statute in certain circumstances (see the warranties about merchantable quality and fitness for purpose referred to below) or they may be 'express' — actually agreed between both sides.

A statement, for example about a horse's soundness, might be a representation (see misrepresentation below) or a warranty or a condition. Common matters of this nature, which have legal connotations include:

Unsoundness. There is a broad legal definition of unsoundness which in simplified terms states:

> A horse is considered to be unsound if, at the time of sale, he has any disease which then or as a result of progression/deterioration (i) diminishes his natural usefulness or (ii) makes him less capable of work or, if as a result of disease or accident, the horse has undergone any alteration of structure which now or as a result of progression/deterioration causes (i) and/or (ii) above.

The term 'unsoundness' may relate not only to the limbs, but to all physiological aspects, such as breathing and circulation.

Vice. A vice is an habitual or temperamental problem that is not deemed to be normal behaviour in the horse, e.g. wind-sucking and rearing.

5) *Merchantable quality*. Section 14 (2) of the 1979 Act states that goods sold must be of merchantable quality, i.e. 'fit for the purpose(s) for which goods of that kind are commonly bought'. This applies to both new and second-hand goods. However, this condition does not apply if, before the contract is made:

(i) Any defects are specifically brought to the attention of the buyer.

(ii) The buyer inspects the goods for defects which his inspection ought to reveal.

The principle of 'caveat emptor' ('let the buyer beware') states that the buyer must be careful in his purchases and examine them for obvious defects.

6) *Fitness for purpose.* Section 14 (3) of the 1979 Act states that 'if the buyer makes known to the seller the purpose for which the goods are required, either by telling him expressly or by implication, there is an implied condition that the goods will be fit for that purpose unless circumstances show that the buyer is not relying on the seller's skill or judgement or that it would be unreasonable for him to do so'. Therefore a yard selling horses must endeavour to provide mounts suitable to the differing skills and requirements of the clientele.

7) *Sale by sample.* Goods such as hay and straw may be ordered by reference to a sample. Section 15 of the 1979 Act states that it is implied that the bulk of the goods will be of the same type and quality as the sample. If this is not so the buyer is entitled to reject the goods, reclaim the purchase price and sue for damages.

8) *Right to sell.* The seller must have the right to sell at the time that ownership passes to the buyer. The basic rule is that someone cannot sell what they do not own, which means that the innocent buyer of stolen goods often has to give them back to the true owner. However, there are several exceptions to this principle, for example sales in 'market overt' which includes some traditional markets and sales by certain people whom the seller has allowed to have possession of the goods.

   If a horse is sold by a dealer on behalf of someone else, the dealer will be acting as the owner's agent. Usually the buyer will be able to assume that the dealer has the necessary authority to sell the horse. The owner will usually be bound by a contract for sale entered into on his behalf by the dealer.

Exclusion clauses

These are clauses excluding or limiting the liability of one party to a contract for breach of contract and may not be effective. Certain implied terms may not be excluded and in some cases exclusion clauses are only enforceable if they are reasonable. A court would consider what was reasonable when the contract was entered into; it would not consider what would be regarded as reasonable in the light of subsequent events.

Misrepresentations

This section should be studied especially closely by those whose business includes buying and selling horses.

A representation is a statement by one side, before a contract is entered into, that induces the other side to enter into the contract.

Misrepresentations are untrue statements which can take several forms:

Fraudulent misrepresentations are knowingly dishonest but are difficult to prove. Once proven the innocent party may either cancel the contract or carry it through. Whichever course of action he takes, he is entitled to claim damages.

Negligent misrepresentations are easier to prove. The maker of these statements must pay damages unless he can prove that he believed the statements to be true up to the time that the contract was made.

Innocent misrepresentations are those made by someone who genuinely believes the statements to be true. The person who enters a contract as a result of an innocent misrepresentation by the other side can cancel the contract and, at the court's discretion, claim damages.

Contractual problems

If you have a problem involving a contract on which you have to consult a solicitor he or she will probably analyse it by following this route:

Is there a contract?

What are its terms?

Is there a breach of contract?

Have you suffered loss as a result of the breach of contract?

Is the type of loss the sort the law will allow you to recover?

Is there an effective exclusion clause?

What loss can be recovered for the breach of contract?

The conclusion to be drawn from this is that it is important that the terms of any contract entered into are clear. Keep any proof of what those terms are in case something goes wrong.

When entering into a contract, say what you mean and mean what you say. Don't assume that the other side knows what you are thinking and don't avoid discussing difficult areas of potential agreement in the hope that they won't cause a problem.

A sample livery contract

One form of contract which is common in the equestrian industry is that between a livery business and the owner of a horse at livery. Too many people, both yard owners and horse owners, pay insufficient attention to this matter, with the result that unpleasant, messy and entirely avoidable disputes arise.

The following is an example of a DIY (Do-it-yourself) livery agreement giving a suggested format. Agreements can be modified to suit the requirements of the individual establishment and should be checked for accuracy by a solicitor before being used. Note that, although it is described as an 'agreement' it does, in fact, constitute a contract.

Do-it-yourself Livery Agreement

This agreement is made on .... 199 .
between .... (the Managers/Proprietor) of .
.... and you ....
.... ('the owner') of .....

Variable Details

Horse: Name   :
             Height :
             Breed   :
             (if known)
             Colour :
             Sex   :
             Age   :
             Freeze mark:

Details of any vices such as crib-biting or chewing wood, wind-sucking, kicking, biting, weaving, rearing, jumping out of fields etc.:

Please give: Your home telephone number: ....

Your work telephone number: ....

Any other numbers upon which you may be contacted: ....

Veterinary surgeon's name: ....

Telephone number: ....

Practice name and address: ....
....

1) In this agreement the term 'horse' includes, where applicable, a horse, pony or other equine.

2) You will pay us £ .... a week, to be paid monthly in advance/arrears. The livery bill must be settled within 14 days of the invoice date. We may increase our charges by giving you not less than .... weeks notice in writing.

3) At the start of this agreement you will pay us a deposit of £ .... which will be returned to you on the termination of this agreement provided all sums due to us have been paid.

4) You authorize us to call out your veterinary surgeon to attend to your horse if we, at our absolute discretion, think it is necessary. This does not impose any obligation upon us to do so. You authorize us to use any

veterinary surgeon in an emergency and to instruct him to take such action as he advises. You are responsible for all charges from any veterinary surgeon, whether called out by yourself or us.

5) You will choose your own farrier to attend to your horse and he will invoice you direct.

6) We will provide you with a stable for your horse, a field in which it may be turned out with others and storage space for a reasonable amount of forage. You will use the stable and field which we from time to time specify.

7) You must:
   (i)   Let us know of any changes to the details given at the start of the contract.
   (ii)   Worm your horse on the first day of this agreement and then on the first day of every other month until this agreement ceases.
   (iii)   Feed your horse properly and make sure that it has clean, fresh water available at all times.
   (iv)   Muck out and bed down properly the stable used by your horse and regularly collect the droppings from the field. If your horse is turned out with others, liaise with the other owners to ensure fair distribution of this chore. If the fields are not kept clear we, the yard owners, shall undertake the task and charge an appropriate fee to each horse owner.
   (v)   Turn out your horse (in appropriate rugs if necessary) and liaise with other owners to avoid leaving one horse out in the field on its own if this is likely to cause distress to that horse.
   (vi)   Groom and exercise your horse appropriately to ensure its physical and mental well-being.
   (vii)   Ensure that your horse's feet are regularly attended to by your farrier (you are responsible for calling him out).
   (viii) Ensure that your horse is vaccinated against equine influenza and tetanus.
   (ix)   Keep the yard and your personal property in it tidy.
   (x)   Let us know if you notice any damage to fencing or stables so that it may be repaired.

8) Unless caused through our negligence or that of our employees, we shall not be liable to you for any injury, illness or death of you or your horse or for any loss of or damage to your personal property however caused. The welfare of your horse is your sole responsibility.

9) We shall not be liable for any loss, injury, damage or death caused by your horse, tack or other property and you shall indemnify us against all actions, proceedings, costs, claims or demands so caused.

10) We require you to be insured against claims by third parties for damage caused by your horse for a minimum of £500,000.

11) We strongly recommend that you take out adequate other insurance

and at all times when riding, wear a fastened crash hat to current BSI standards.

12) You may exercise your horse in the area provided and use the jumps provided. This is done entirely at your own risk and, as stated in Clause 8, we shall not be liable for any loss, injury, damage or death to yourself, your horse or any other person.

13) The livery contract may be terminated by either you or us on 28 days written notice. On or before the expiry of the notice all outstanding sums of money owed to us must be paid before your property is removed.

14) If the owner is more than one person all obligations shall be joint and several.

Horse Owner's Copy: . . . .
                                             Yard Owner

Yard Owner's Copy: . . . .
                                             Horse Owner

A livery agreement made in respect of a full or working livery could consist of everything above, excluding those points relating to the duties carried out by the DIY owner, and including details about general care, turning out, clipping, trimming, schooling, exercising, use of the school, preparation for shows and/or hunting and transportation.

THE LAW OF TORT

The law of tort is concerned with civil wrongs other than a breach of contract which are not punishable by the State. There are many different sorts of tort, the most relevant of which are discussed below.

Negligence

Negligence is a breach of duty of care as a result of the defendant either omitting to do something that a reasonable person would do and/or doing something that a reasonable person would not do. In a claim of negligence it must be established that:

1) The defendant owed a duty of care to the claimant. (Everyone has a duty to take reasonable care not to harm others who they can reasonably foresee might be harmed by their action.)

2) The defendant was in breach of that duty.

3) The claimant suffered consequent loss. This is generally damage in the form of physical harm, but may also mean financial loss.

Equestrian establishments operating as a business cannot limit their liability for death or personal injury resulting from negligence, because of provisions imposed by the Unfair Contract Terms Act 1977. This Act applies to liabilities arising from 'things done or to be done by a person in the course of business' and the occupation of premises used for 'business purposes'. A sign displayed excluding liability is invalid. Note also that the owner/employer is liable for the actions of any employees in the event of an accident occurring due to their negligent (or, indeed, other tortious) behaviour.

Voluntary assumption of risk

There may be instances whereby the rule 'Volenti non fit injuria' (where there is consent there is no injury) can be applied to limit liability. It must be established that the claimant freely and voluntarily assumed the risk, for example spectators at a cross-country competition would probably have no claim in the event of a fallen rider's loose horse cantering into them. This rule never applies to employees as any risks involved are not considered to have been voluntarily accepted.

Trespass

To enter someone's land without consent or lawful authority is trespass. The occupier is legally entitled to encourage the trespasser to leave 'using no more force than is necessary' if they will not leave freely, but the use of physical persuasion or threats is not to be recommended (as it could constitute an assault). The occupier may sue the trespasser but this is generally not worthwhile unless actual damage has occurred.

Private nuisance

This is an unlawful interference with a person's use or enjoyment of land or some right over or in connection with it. The nuisance may be noise, smells or similar and must be substantial or have caused actual damage before the courts may award damages and/or impose an injunction to stop the nuisance.

'THE OCCUPIERS' LIABILITY ACTS 1957 AND 1984.

These Acts are concerned with the legal duty of the occupier to protect the well-being of all visitors, whatever their nature, to the property.

The 1957 Act covers all lawful visitors who have permission, either expressed or implied, to be on the property. The responsibilities of the occupier are defined 'as a duty to take such care as in all the circumstances of the case is reasonable to see that the visitor will be reasonably safe in using the premises for which he is invited or permitted by the occupier to be there'.

The occupier must be aware of all potential dangers and take steps to prevent accidents from occurring. For example in a stable yard, young children are inclined to approach horses with no idea of potential consequences and dangers. Every effort must be made to prevent young children from running around the yard unsupervised.

The 1984 Act covers all uninvited visitors including trespassers. If the occupier knows:

1) There is a danger or has reasonable grounds to believe a danger exists, or

2) has reasonable grounds to believe that an entrant either is

or might come into the vicinity of the danger, or

3) that the risk of injury resulting from the danger is one against which in all circumstances of the case the occupier can reasonably be expected to offer the uninvited entrant some protection,

he or she is legally bound to 'take such care as is reasonable in all the circumstances of the case to see that he does not suffer injury (i.e. death or personal injury, not property damage) on the premises by reason of the danger concerned.'

THE RIDING ESTABLISHMENTS ACTS 1964 AND 1970

These Acts require that a licence is obtained from the local council if the establishment hires out horses or gives lessons in return for remuneration, even if only on a part-time basis. The applicant must:

1) Have planning permission to use the premises as a riding establishment.

2) Have public liability insurance to the sum specified by the local council. There are occasionally difficulties here as some insurance companies will only offer cover upon receipt of a copy of the Riding School Licence. Diplomatic negotiations are then called for!

3) Be 18 years of age or more, or be a body corporate.

4) Not be disqualified from keeping a riding school, pet shop, boarding kennels, dog or having custody of animals.

5) Satisfy the local authority of suitability to run the establishment either through examination qualifications or depth of experience. If formal qualifications are held, the applicant need not refer to his or her experience.

The premises and all horses and ponies upon it used for hire and/or instructional purposes are thoroughly checked by an authorized veterinary surgeon, who is generally accompanied by an inspector from the local council. The inspection is very thorough and covers the following aspects:

The health and fitness of all horses and ponies used in connection with the business. They are examined and trotted up to test for lameness. In the event of any abnormalities, such as saddle sores, the vet will instruct the owner not to use the animal until completely healed.

Suitability of horses or ponies for the purposes for which they are kept. Details of any youngsters (three years old and under) must be recorded on a register which is available for inspection by an authorized officer from the local council at any time.

The condition of all horses' feet and shoes. Feet must be properly trimmed and, if shod, shoes must be well fitted and in good condition.

Adequate provision of veterinary first aid and human first aid kits.

The means of controlling infectious/contagious ailments. It is necessary to have a functional isolation box.

The suitability of stables. Drainage, ventilation, safety, size and lighting are all considered.

The provision of adequate food, water and bedding.

Adequate storage for forage, bedding, stable equipment and saddlery.

The provision of adequate pasture, water, shelter and supplementary feed to all animals living out at grass.

All horses must be regularly exercised, groomed and rested as appropriate.

The provision of a fire point, equipped with suitable fire-fighting equipment and a large, clear display giving the information as to action to be taken in the event of fire.

The supervision of persons hiring a horse. Unless the licence holder considers that a person is competent enough to ride unaccompanied, clients must always be supervised by someone aged fifteen years or over.

There must always be a responsible person aged sixteen or more present at the establishment during working hours.

Any person convicted of running an unlicensed riding school or hacking/trekking centre may be fined or imprisoned and disqualified from obtaining or holding a licence. Livery yards are not covered by the The Riding Establishments Acts, so do not need a licence.

THE ANIMALS ACT 1971

Owners of animals have a duty of care applied to them, the details of which are specified by The Animals Act 1971.

Strict liability, that is liability without fault, is imposed upon owners when their animals stray onto someone else's land. The landowner has the right to keep and sell any unclaimed animals and seek expenses from the original owner. Liability is for damage done to the land or any property upon it. Generally it is the owner's obligation to keep the animals fenced in, rather than the landowner's duty to keep them out.

An exception to this rule occurs when animals are grazed on unfenced common land and have a lawful right to be on the highway − should they stray onto someone else's property negligence must be proved. For example an occupier of a house in the New Forest must keep his or her garden stockproof. If failing to do so, any damage incurred could be deemed to be his or her own fault.

Unless grazing on common land, owners are under a duty of care to prevent their animals from straying onto the highway. Liability is not, however, strict and the owner is only found liable if he or she has not exercised reasonable care to prevent the animals from straying, for example through not providing adequate fencing.

The owner of an animal is liable for damages, either to property or personal injury if:

1) The damage is of the kind which the animal was likely to

cause if not restrained, or which if caused by the animal was likely to be severe.

2) The likelihood of the damage or its being severe must be due to characteristics of the animal which are not normally found in animals of the same species except at particular times or in particular circumstances.

3) These characteristics are known to the keeper of the animal, an employee or a member of the household aged sixteen years or more.

In the event of these three criteria being met the owner is liable regardless of whose fault it is.

3

INSURANCE

It is advisable to seek advice of a reputable insurance broker when reviewing insurance requirements. Whichever companies/brokers are chosen it is important to:

Check their record for prompt payment of claims.

Read the small print — check the policies carefully, preferably with your solicitor, to make sure you are receiving the cover you think you are.

Ensure that you have sufficient cover — insure for full replacement value and consequential loss.

COMPULSORY INSURANCE

There are some insurances which are compulsory in a commercial riding establishment. These are:

Employer's liability

Under the Employer's Liability (Compulsory Insurance) Act 1969, it is a legal requirement of all businesses which employ staff to hold this insurance. It covers legal claims by employees in relation to personal injuries or damage to their property whilst at work.

Public liability

It is essential to have adequate public liability insurance when applying for a riding school licence. It covers death, injury or illness caused to a member of the public as a result of defects in the premises, the services offered or negligence by either the proprietor or staff.

All insurance policies should be read thoroughly. There may, for example, be clauses stating that cover is only valid when riders are wearing correctly fitted headgear which meets BSI standards. As an added precaution, members of the public should not be encouraged to wander around the yard. Notices should be displayed instructing them to report to the reception area and to keep small children under control. Many people are unaware of the dangers involved, so a notice warning them not to feed the horses titbits would be prudent.

Motor vehicle

A minimum of third party cover is needed on all vehicles. This covers other vehicles and people whilst a fully comprehensive policy covers the replacement value of the insured vehicle as well. Vehicles used for hire or reward, such as horseboxes, will be subject to amendments on the policy.

NON-COMPULSORY INSURANCE

Non-compulsory policies which are worth considering include personal accident, property and contents damage, and business interruption.

Personal Accident

It is important that self-employed persons are covered in respect of financial security in the event of their sustaining a disabling illness or accident. Employees involved in risky tasks, such as breaking-in youngsters, may be wise to take out a personal accident policy. Employees would not be covered by their Employer's Liability policy if an accident occurred outside the hours of work, for example if exercising their own horse at lunchtime.

Property and contents

All buildings should be insured against damage by fire or adverse weather conditions, such as gales and floods. Cover should be based on *rebuilding* costs and not market value. It is compulsory for all mortgaged properties to be insured.

All contents, including tack, should be insured at replacement value. If large quantities of hay and straw are stored, this too should be insured.

Business interruption

This covers consequential loss of profits as a result of some interruption to the running of the business, resulting from factors such as flood damage, outbreak of disease etc.

Horses

There is a wide range of insurance policies aimed at the horse owner. Cover can vary from simple third party protection to complete cover including loss of use, vet's fees, loss by theft or straying etc.

4

EMPLOYING PEOPLE

Once staff have been taken on, the business owner becomes an employer and is from then on under certain legal obligations as defined by The Employment Protection Consolidation Act (1978). The Inland Revenue produce a leaflet entitled *Thinking of Taking Someone on?* which gives information about the taxation of employees.

STATUTORY DUTIES OF AN EMPLOYER

These are:

1) To comply with The Employment Protection Consolidation Act 1978.

2) To provide safe systems of work as detailed in the Health and Safety at Work Act 1974.

3) To keep adequate wages records and deduct PAYE tax and National Insurance contributions. This involves informing the tax office, calculating period tax and National Insurance contributions and submitting an annual return.

4) To pay tax and National Insurance contributions to the Inland Revenue each month.

5) To provide Statutory Maternity Pay and Statutory Sick Pay as appropriate.

6) To notify the tax office when an employee leaves (providing a form P45).

CONTRACT OF EMPLOYMENT (SEE ALSO LAW OF CONTRACT)

The Employment Protection Consolidation Act 1978 requires that any employee working sixteen hours or more per week must be given a written statement of his or her terms of employment within thirteen weeks of starting work. This statement must cover the aspects set out in the Act.

A copy of this statement should be kept by the employer. The employee should be asked to sign this copy which implies he or she has received the written statement. However, the employee's signature does not imply that the terms and conditions specified have been accepted; indeed the employee is not *legally obliged to* sign the statement.

Any adjustments must be made in writing and signed to the effect that the employee has received a copy within one month of the introduction of any alterations. This written statement is not deemed to be a contract but is taken as strong evidence of the terms of the contract of employment. It should include the following details:

Name, address and relevant information about the employer and employee.

Job specification — title and details of duties to be undertaken.

Date of commencement of employment.

Rate of remuneration and when this is to be paid, i.e. weekly; monthly.

Hours of work.

Accommodation arrangements if applicable.

Holiday benefits (this should include holiday entitlements upon termination of employment).

Pay during sickness or injury.

Health plan or pension if applicable.

Fringe benefits such as keep of a horse. (When discussing fringe benefits they must be itemized and quantified in monetary terms then, in the event of the benefit ceasing, the value of that benefit is made up in cash.)

Length of notice of termination of employment (which must not be less than the statutory minimum).

Grievance procedure — this should include details of:

1) The disciplinary rules applicable to the employee.

2) The details of the person to whom the employee can apply should he or she be dissatisfied with any disciplinary decision.

3) The details of the person the employee can approach regarding any grievance concerning employment.

Under the Employment Protection Consolidation Act 1978, all employees must receive an itemized pay statement. This statement must show:

1) The gross amount earned before deductions.

2) Details of all deductions, such as National Insurance.

3) Details of all negotiable deductions, such as board, horse keep etc.

4) The net amount earned after deductions.

Dismissal

Any person who works sixteen hours or more a week, and has been employed for two years or more, is protected from unfair dismissal. In calculating the two year period you should take into account the notice period. If someone works from eight to sixteen hours a week they are protected once they have been employed for five years or more.

An employee may sue his or her employer in the County Court for breach of contract or complain to an industrial tribunal if he or she claims unfair dismissal or is redundant and has not been paid the due amount of redundancy money.

When dismissing an employee, consideration has to be given to any breach of contract by the employer as well as liability for redundancy or unfair dismissal. Therefore, expert advice should always be sought before dismissing an employee: if an employer wants to sack an employee without notice it is especially important that the advice is sought immediately.

Working pupil arrangements

If a student is to train at a centre as a working pupil, the conditions must be discussed and clearly agreed. A contract should be prepared which is signed and accepted by the employer/trainer and the student. In the case of a young student (under eighteen) it is advisable to discuss the contract with the parents also.

The working pupil arrangement is very common throughout the equestrian industry. From the point of view of both pupil and trainer, a well thought out and agreed contract offers some degree of protection against recriminations at a later date if things don't quite go to plan.

A working contract should cover the following points:

1) The duration of the training course (it may be open ended).

2) Whether there is to be a trial period.

3) The aim of the course, that is the pupil's target. For example, a specific qualification.

4) A broad description of the duties involved.

5) What training the pupil can expect to receive in equitation, stable management and instructing.

6) Hours to be worked each day.

7) Days off including weekends, bank holidays and annual holiday.

8) Whether days spent competing, hunting or taking exams count as part of the working week or as days off.

9) Any financial arrangements.

10) Other perks including accommodation, food and keep of a horse.

11) Who applies and pays for any examinations.

12) What notice is required to terminate the contract.

Further advice may be sought from the British Horse Society.

Statutory maternity pay

A pregnant employee is entitled to eighteen weeks Statutory Maternity Pay (SMP) either before or after the expected week of confinement (EWC). However, SMP can be paid no earlier than the eleventh week before the EWC. The employee is not eligible for SMP while she is at work.

Statutory sick pay (SSP)

This social security payment is also made through the wage packet — the onus is on the employer to keep all records. The amount to be paid is calculated on earnings and is paid for the period of incapacity for work (PIW). This situation is reached on the fourth day of absence. After forty days the employee receives SSP direct from the Department of Social Security.

HEALTH AND SAFETY AT WORK

All employers have a legal responsibility to ensure the health and safety of their employees so far as is reasonably practical. The Health and Safety at Work Act 1974 compels employers to maintain safe equipment, premises and procedures. The conditions of the Act encompass employers, employees and all visitors to the establishment.

With regard to equestrian businesses, the Act is enforced by the Agricultural Inspectorate, a representative of which inspects equestrian establishments to ensure compliance with the appropriate conditions. Failure to comply may lead to the Inspectorate imposing a Notice upon the person responsible. An Improvement Notice requires that the offending person remedy the contravened provision within a specified period. A Prohibition Notice may be issued when the Inspectorate deems that a work activity may involve a risk of serious personal injury, and can be enforced immediately.

Failure to obey these Notices is a criminal offence.

The health and safety policy statement

Under the Health and Safety at Work Act, an employer of five or more people is obliged to prepare and display a written statement of the business's policy in respect of health and safety at work. This policy must be kept updated and amended as necessary. All members of staff must be aware of, and familiar with, the policy. The Health and Safety Executive has issued a booklet called *Writing your Health and Safety Policy Statement*, which offers advice on the contents of the policy.

The policy must state the intention of the employer and employees to comply with the statutory provisions and thus ensure, through good communications, the co-operation of the workforce and the enforcement of safe routines. The completed policy must be signed by the employer, a partner or senior director of the business.

Any persons responsible for overseeing health and safety at work must be well prepared and trained to carry out the task. Furthermore, practical arrangements must be made to ensure health and safety at work. These arrangements involve:

1) Identifying all potential hazards and their management. (For example, handling weedkiller).

2) Listing the rules and practices for avoiding accidents.

3) Explaining the procedures in the event of fire, injury or other emergencies.

First aid and occupational health

The Health and Safety (First Aid) Regulations 1981 give minimum accepted standards for the provision of first aid. These are laid out in the booklet *First Aid at Work*, obtainable from HMSO. Consideration should also be given to the following:

All establishments should have at least one trained first aider, who should preferably have obtained a 'First Aid at Work' certificate.

All persons involved with horses should be immunized against tetanus. An effective rodent control programme should be carried out as necessary and, in order to reduce the risk of contracting the rodent-borne Weil's disease, any person working in a contaminated area must be advised to wear protective clothing and to change clothes and wash scrupulously afterwards.

Dust and fungal spores found in hay and bedding can cause respiratory problems such as 'farmer's lung'. Therefore, dust should be kept to a minimum wherever possible. If staff are working in an unavoidably dusty atmosphere, ensure that suitable respiratory filter masks are worn.

Further information on first aid procedures is given in Chapter Five of this book.

Sanitary conveniences and washing facilities

Where male and female workers are employed, provided that the total number of employees does not exceed five, one sanitary convenience is adequate. Where the workforce exceeds five, separate facilities should be provided in relation to the numbers of workers employed as follows:

Numbers employed	WC Requirement
1–5 total	1 shared
1–15 males and females	1 each for males and females
16–30 males	2, or 1 plus 1 urinal
16–30 females	2 WC
For every additional 25 (or fewer) males	1 WC or urinal, providing that there is an equal or greater number of WCs than urinals
For every additional 25 (or fewer) females	1 WC

Sanitary facilities must be under cover, partitioned off for privacy, have adequate lighting and have proper doors and fastenings. They must not communicate directly with a room or place in which people are working. The interior of a room housing a sanitary convenience must not be visible — even with the door open — by members of the opposite sex, and urinals must not be visible from any place where people work or pass. Sanitary facilities must be maintained, kept clean and have an adequate supply of paper. Where female facilities are provided, suitable means for the disposal of sanitary dressings should be available.

Wherever it is reasonably practicable to do so, water closets or urinals with a water flushing system and a drainage system to a sewer or cesspool, should be provided. Where this is not practicable, a chemical or dry packaging toilet may be used. The Buildings Regulations lay down standards of construction for drainage systems and sanitary conveniences which must be complied with.

Washing facilities should be provided in the following minimum numbers:

1−15 workers	1 washbasin
16−50 workers	2 washbasins
For every additional 25 (or fewer) workers	1 washbasin

Washbasins must include clean running hot (or warm) and cold water, soap (liquid, powder or solid) and drying facilities (continuous linen towels, disposable paper towels, automatic hot air dryers etc.). The facilities must be conveniently accessible to the workforce and must be kept clean and well maintained.

Staff training

The Health and Safety at Work Act 1974 states that employees must receive instruction, training and supervision in order to carry out their job safely. Staff training should concentrate on safe systems of work with emphasis placed on safety and care rather than speed when performing a task.

Any new employee or voluntary helper will need close supervision until the employer is satisfied that he or she is competent. The level of supervision will depend in all instances upon the employee's age, experience and level of training.

Further information on staff training is given in Chapter Six of this book.

SAFETY CHECKS

Safe working practices should be observed not only when they are statutory requirements, but at all times, in the interests of all concerned. The following is a brief summary of main safety points:

In the yard

Equipment must always be put away in its correct place. All machinery, for example hay-making equipment, should be guarded as appropriate and used only by someone trained in its correct use.

Store rodenticides, veterinary medications, disinfectants etc. in a safe place. Drugs should not be accessible to unauthorized persons and unwanted drugs, syringes etc. must be safely disposed of.

All electrical wiring must be kept up to date and in good order. All wires, switches etc. must be sealed to prevent horses from tampering with them. Rodents will also chew electrical wires. Use circuit breaker plugs whenever electrical equipment such as clippers are in use.

Buildings must be well made from safe materials and maintained in good condition. Ensure that the yard is sufficiently well lit when in use after dark.

Fixtures and fittings should be kept to a minimum. They must always have smooth rounded edges.

All glass windows must be protected by a wire grille.

Doors must always open outwards, be robust and have two bolts. When shutting, always make sure that the bottom bolts are fastened.

When leading through doorways, always ensure that the door cannot swing onto the horse as he walks through. Wear gloves when leading or lungeing to avoid the risk of rope burns should the horse suddenly pull backwards or away.

In icy conditions, spread salt on the yard to help prevent slipping. Repair any uneven paving, potholes, broken steps etc. and keep all passages and pathways clear of obstructions.

Never allow inexperienced people to handle the horses unsupervised.

Always keep horses apart whilst standing in the yard to prevent kicking.

Always tie up safely to a securely fitted ring using a weak link and a quick-release knot.

The yard gate must be kept shut at all times.

Nobody should use faulty equipment, such as clippers. They should report it and ensure it is repaired. If linseed/barley boilers are used, follow manufacturers' instructions, keep well maintained and inform everyone of the dangers of handling the boiled food.

Only trained, experienced staff should assist farriers and vets. This applies especially to vets using portable X-ray equipment: The Ionising Radiations Regulations 1985 apply to this type of equipment.

In the field

Always check gates and fences, repairing them soundly as needed. Use only safe forms of fencing: avoid barbed wire.

When turning out, lead the horse in a headcollar into the field. Turn the horse's head toward you and remove the headcollar, stepping backwards as you do so. By keeping his hindquarters into the field this reduces the risk of your being kicked in the event of him galloping off.

Turning out in a bridle is risky; should the horse pull away quickly, the bit can get caught in his teeth. Some strong horses, however, need to be led in a bridle.

Always keep the field clear of litter, rabbit holes, machinery, loose wiring, low branches etc.

Be observant. When turning horses out together watch for bullying. Some combinations just don't get on and are best turned out separately.

Gates on unsupervised fields should be padlocked at both ends as thieves will lift gates from their hinges.

Horses should ideally be freeze-marked to deter thieves.

Whilst riding

The yard manager/owner has a legal responsibility to ensure that all equipment used by horses and riders is in safe condition and meets current British Standards. Therefore, all tack and equipment used must be kept clean, in good condition and must be well fitting. Should an item of equipment be faulty and cause an accident, the yard owner may be liable to prosecution for negligence.

The rider must wear correct footwear; riding boots, as opposed to trainers or wellingtons. When handling horses, footwear with a reinforced toe is the safest choice.

A crash cap or hard hat must always be worn with a correctly fitted harness. The recommended hats are jockey skull cap BSI Standard 4472 or riding hat type 6473.

Keep jewellery to a safe minimum. Loop earrings, large rings and bangles can easily become caught up and cause serious injury. Necklaces can present a choking hazard in the event of a fall.

If riding in dull conditions where visibility may be poor, wear a reflective tabard to help motorists see you. It is not advisable to ride at dusk, but if you have no alternative, use stirrup lights and reflective strips on your horse. Fluorescent bands to go around the horse's tail and legs are available.

Never hack out if the roads are icy unless you are certain that you can ride on the verges. Apart from the risk of the horse slipping, motorists are not always in full control of their vehicles on ice and snow.

If riding a young or nervous horse, try to go with an older animal who will set a good example. This can help when trying to pass anything that horses consider to be 'spooky'.

Children must always be accompanied by a responsible person and should ideally ride traffic-proof, well behaved ponies. Keep group rides as small as is practical and always ensure that the weakest rider is never expected to do more than he or she is capable of.

Ride in single file on the left-hand side of the road. Remember to give clear signals if there are any other road users about. Always thank drivers who slow down for you.

Have a thorough knowledge and understanding of the Highway and Country Codes.

Fire prevention

Because of the large amount of hay, straw and shavings stored, stable yards are particularly susceptible to the danger of fire. Following these rules can help to prevent a fire:

Enforce a strict **No Smoking** rule, with signs to this effect easily visible around the yard.

Keep all electric wires in good order, preferably protected against damage from chewing by horses and rodents and with watertight PVC coverings.

Remove dust and cobwebs from all light bulbs and ensure that lights are covered with a wire mesh if there is the slightest chance that a horse could reach them.

There is a danger that damp hay will heat up in the stack — particularly if new. Always stack new hay loosely to allow air to circulate between the bales. Never leave glass bottles lying near hay or straw as, apart from the obvious danger of being trodden on, the effect of sunlight on glass can cause a direct heat capable of starting a fire.

Store flammable materials such as gas bottles, petrol cans, paint etc. in a completely separate shed away from the main buildings.

Keep the buildings and yard free of litter which can easily help a fire to spread more quickly. Never allow bonfires or fireworks near the yard.

Any electrical applicances used must be in safe working order and correctly wired into a properly fused plug. All wiring and appliances should be checked regularly by a qualified electrician. Never run an extension cable over hay or straw; coiled electrical cables generate a lot of heat when in use.

Ask the local Fire Prevention Officer to visit the yard. He will advise on any danger areas and the equipment needed to fight a fire.

The fire point

Every yard should have a fire point. In a commercial establishment it is a legal requirement — a riding school licence will not be granted unless the fire point is satisfactory. It should be in a prominent position — preferably sited so it may be seen by a passer-by. Large yards may need more than one fire point.

The fire point should display a notice containing the information shown at the top of the next page:

Anyone handling horses in the yard must be aware that:

Headcollars must always be in a clearly visible position — never locked away.

In the case of a horse not wanting to leave his stable you should cover his head with a wet blanket or similar to blindfold him and try to lead him out. (As horses feel secure in their

ACTION TO BE TAKEN IN CASE OF FIRE

The nearest telephones may be found at ......

The address of this establishment is ......

Dial 999 — request Fire Brigade

Sound alarm — Ring bell

The name and telephone no. of the owner is ....

Move horses in greatest danger first, using headcollars if time permits

If you have no time — open stable doors to release horses

Put horses into paddocks or indoor/outdoor school[1]

Shut both doors of empty stables[2]

Tackle fire without endangering life

---

[1] Loose horses charging around could hinder the Fire Brigade and get loose onto the road
[2] This helps to prevent the spread of the fire as well as stopping a terrified horse from returning to his stable

stables they may be unwilling to walk out even though they may be in danger.)

The fire point should also consist of:

An alarm bell or triangle.

At least two water fire extinguishers and two foam ones — ask the Fire Officer for advice.

At least two water buckets.

At least two sand-filled buckets.

A full water tank — this may need to have salt added to prevent it from freezing in winter.

An axe.

A hosepipe already attached to a tap — in an emergency you would waste precious time trying to attach the hose to the tap. In winter be sure that the hose is empty to avoid ice forming inside. The hose must be long enough to reach the furthest building and should be regularly tested for leaks. Be sure that there is good water pressure from the tap.

In a busy yard try to practise your fire drill occasionally and make sure that everyone knows how to operate the extinguishers. Fire extinguishers must be serviced regularly in order to be effective — they must be protected in winter months to prevent freezing.

If there is no fire hydrant or large pond in close proximity it may be worth considering the installation of a hydrant.

Wherever several horses are stabled in one building, there must be more than one wide, easily accessible exit.

In circumstances where hostel accommodation is offered, the Fire Precautions Act 1971 is applicable. Such premises must be in possession of a current Fire Certificate and are subject to inspection by the Local Authority.

5

ACCIDENT PROCEDURE

When it comes to safety, the list of dos and don'ts is endless. So much depends really upon the 'horse sense' that the handler has acquired through experience. Unfortunately, though, accidents do happen and on the following pages we shall discuss how best to handle the different situations.

Note, however that the information given within this book cannot attempt to replace training given by a skilled and qualified first aid instructor. It cannot be stressed enough that any person involved with horses should attend a public first aid course and obtain a certificate in first aid.

Courses are held regularly by the St John Ambulance and The British Red Cross Society.

FIRST AID KIT

Every tack room should have a first aid kit for the humans as well as one for the horses. The kit must never be locked away. It should contain:

An assortment of sterilized dressings — 3 medium, 1 large and 1 extra large.

A box of waterproof dressings (sticking plasters).
2 triangular bandages.
1 spool of adhesive plaster.
Absorbent cotton wool.
6 large safety pins.
Antiseptic ointment.
1 sterile eye pad with bandage.
Scissors.
2 crepe roller bandages.

The first aid box must be well maintained, kept clean and up to date.

A SIMPLE FALL

One of the hazards of riding is that occasionally one becomes airborne at an unexpected moment. Should this happen to a colleague or pupil whilst riding you must halt the rest of the ride. Organize somebody to catch the loose horse to prevent him from injuring himself or causing another accident. Check that the rider feels all right and if so let him or her remount. It is better for the sake of confidence to remount as soon as realistically possible. However, ensure that the rider is not still partially incapacitated by, for example, the after-effects of being 'winded'.

Even the most harmless-looking fall could cause a bang on the head. If the rider has hit his or her head and complains of headaches or dizziness then he or she should be taken to hospital for an X-ray and general check-up.

DEALING WITH A SERIOUS FALL

The aims of first aid are:

1) To preserve life.

2) To prevent deterioration in the casualty's condition.

3) To promote recovery.

Your first step is to assess the situation calmly:

1) Is the casualty in any further danger? For example, a rider who has fallen into a water or mud-filled ditch may be in danger of drowning.

2) If the accident has occurred on the road, organize bystanders to control the traffic and send for the emergency services. If the horse has been injured a vet will be required.

3) Establish whether the casualty is conscious or not. Do this by speaking loudly to them and very gently shake them by the shoulder.

The unconscious casualty

Having established that the casualty is unconscious you must ensure that the airway is open, check for breathing and a pulse. This is often referred to as the ABC of resuscitation – Airway, Breathing and Circulation.

A. Airway
If the casualty is lying on his or her back the airway may be blocked due to the tongue dropping back and blocking the throat. To open the airway, scoop out any obstructions such as broken teeth or dentures. Leave well fitting dentures in place as they can help when administering artificial ventilation. Place two fingers under the casualty's chin and the other hand on his or her forehead. Carefully tilt the head well back.

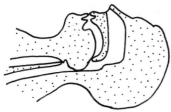 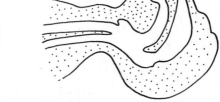

Figure 1. Opening a blocked airway.

a) The airway is blocked, the casualty cannot breathe.

b) Tilt the head back and the chin up to allow free passage of air; the airway is opened.

B. Breathing

To check for breathing, place your face near the casualty's mouth and *look* for chest movements, *listen* for sounds of breathing and *feel* for breath on your cheek. Do this for five seconds.

Figure 2. Look, listen and feel for breathing

C. Circulation

To check for a pulse, with the casualty's head still tilted back, feel for the gap between the Adam's apple and the 'strap' muscle where the carotid pulse may be felt. Feel for five seconds with your index and middle fingers to decide whether or not a pulse is present.

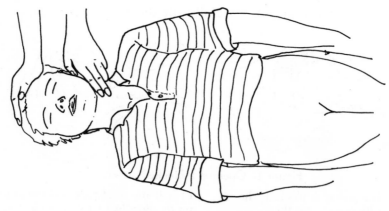

Figure 3. Feeling for the carotid pulse

The crash cap

Do not remove the crash cap unless it is absolutely necessary. Ideally it should be left on – clumsy removal can lead to further damage, particularly if neck and/or head injuries have occurred.

If the crash cap is preventing artificial ventilation from being administered, then it may have to be removed, although undoing the chin strap only should allow artificial ventilation to be carried out without removing the cap in most instances.

If it *is* essential to remove the crash cap, undo the chin strap, force the sides of the cap apart and, while someone else constantly supports the head and neck, carefully lift the helmet upwards and backwards.

There may be a medical card inside the crash cap containing important information. Ensure that the ambulance staff or doctor see it if the cap has been removed before they arrive.

The body protector

If a body protector is worn it, too, should be left fastened unless it is interfering with breathing, preventing you from seeing the chest rise or interfering with external chest compression; in these cases it can be unzipped at the front but left on the casualty.

The recovery position

If the unconscious casualty is breathing unaided, he or she must be placed in the recovery position to prevent the tongue from blocking the throat and to prevent the inhalation of vomit.

Use the following method:

1) Kneel beside the casualty and ensure that the airway is open by tilting the head and lifting the chin.
   Straighten both legs.
   Place the arm nearer you at right angles to the casualty's body, elbow bent and palm uppermost.

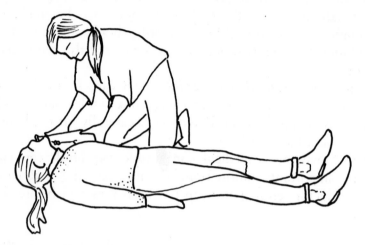

Figure 4a. Method of putting a casualty into the recovery position

2) Bring the further arm across the casualty's chest and hold the hand, palm outwards, against the casualty's nearer cheek.

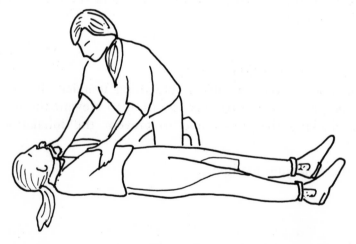

Figure 4b.

3) Use your other hand to take hold of the casualty's further thigh and pull the knee up.

4) Keeping his or her hand pressed against the cheek, pull at the thigh to roll the casualty onto his or her side, facing you.

Figure 4c.

5) Tilt the head back to ensure that the airway remains open. Keep the hand beneath the cheek to assist in this.

6) Ensure that the hip and knee of the upper leg are both at right angles to the body — this will help stop the casualty rolling forwards.

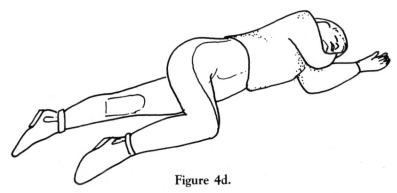

Figure 4d.

7) If not already done, call an ambulance. While waiting for expert help, check breathing and pulse frequently.

Modification of the recovery position
In the event of the unconscious casualty having broken limbs
and/or spinal injuries, the recovery position will need to
be modified.

Extra helpers will be needed, if possible, to turn the casualty.
One helper steadies the head by placing their hands over the
casualty's ears. Maintain support until skilled help arrives, but
do not pull on the neck.

Another helper puts the casualty into the preparatory position
as described earlier then he or she rolls the casualty's body as
the first helper turns the head. *It is imperative that the head and
trunk are constantly aligned to minimize the risk of damage to
the spinal cord.*

Once in this position, maintain the support, manually if
possible. If help has not already been summoned, the helper
must do so. Use rolled blankets, coats or similar to prop the
casualty to prevent his or her body from moving. The head
support must not be removed.

If limbs are broken and cannot be bent, use helpers or rolled
blankets as support.

Artificial ventilation

If the casualty is not breathing, artificial ventilation must be
commenced promptly. Without oxygen, permanent brain
damage and death may occur within three to four minutes.

1) The casualty will need to be turned onto his or her back if
   not already there.
   Assume that there may be neck and/or spinal injury and,
   if possible, have assistants to help turn the casualty very
   carefully.
   Keep the head turning with the body to minimize movement.
   Provided you exercise great care, it is preferable to take the
   risk of turning the casualty in order to administer artificial
   ventilation. Remember that you *have* to turn the casualty to
   do this — if a person is not breathing they will die.

2) Ensure that the airway is open as previously described.

3) Open the casualty's mouth and pinch their nose. Take a full breath, seal their mouth with yours and breathe firmly enough to make the casualty's chest rise.
Watch to see the chest rise.
Remove your lips and allow the chest to fall.
Continue at your normal breathing rate.

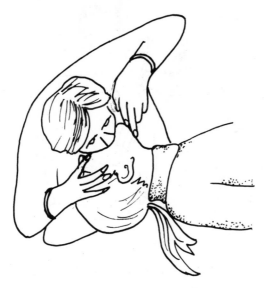

Figure 5. Administering artificial ventilation

4) If the chest does not rise, check that the airway is sufficiently open and is not blocked by an obstruction.
Check that the nostrils are closed completely and that your mouth makes a firm seal around the casualty's.

Chest compression

If there is no pulse the heart has stopped beating. The blood you are oxygenating through mouth to mouth ventilation must be circulated around the body cells, in particular to the brain.

Chest compressions can be applied to force blood through the heart and around the body. This is *always* combined with artificial ventilation and is known as cardio-pulmonary resuscitation (CPR).

1) The casualty must be lying on his or her back on a firm surface.
Place the heel of one hand on the breastbone two fingers' width away from the point at which the lower ribs meet at the breastbone.

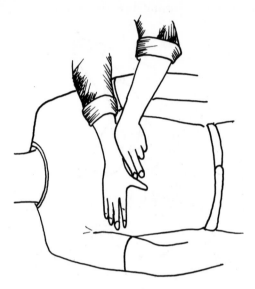

Figure 6. Finding the position for chest compression

The heel of the hand is placed two fingers' width from the lower end of the breastbone.

2) Cover this hand with the heel of the other and interlock your fingers. Keep your fingers off the chest.

3) Lean well forward over the casualty, keep your arms straight, press down on the breastbone to depress it 4–5 cm (1½–2 in) then release the pressure without taking your hands off the casualty's chest.

4) Repeat the compressions at the rate of 60–80 per minute. Count 'one and two and three. . . .' and so on to help keep time and rhythm.

5) In young children under the age of six, use one hand only at a rate of 100 compressions per minute, depressing the chest by 2.5–3.5 cm (1–1½ in).

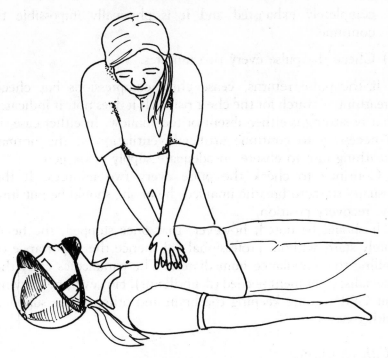

Figure 7. Administering chest compression

The sequence of cardio-pulmonary resuscitation (CPR)

If the casualty is not breathing and has no pulse you must commence CPR immediately.

If alone

1) Dial 999 and call for an ambulance immediately.

2) Ensure that the airway is open and give two breaths of artifical ventilation.

3) Move your hands to the casualty's chest and give fifteen chest compressions.

4) Repeat the process and do not stop until (i) expert help arrives, or (ii) the casualty's pulse returns or (iii) you are

completely exhausted and it is physically impossible to continue.

5) Check the pulse every two minutes.

If the pulse returns, cease chest compressions but check breathing – watch for the chest rising. If it does not, it indicates that breathing is either absent or too shallow. In either case, it is necessary to continue artificial ventilation at the normal breathing rate to ensure an adequate supply of oxygen.

Continue to check the pulse every two minutes. If the casualty starts to breathe unaided, he or she should be put into the recovery position.

It should be noted, however, that once stopped, the heart rarely starts without professional aid, hence the importance of calling the ambulance immediately. The paramedics carry the specialist equipment needed (defibrillator). However, by carrying out CPR you are keeping the brain and other tissues supplied with oxygen.

With assistance

1) One person calls the ambulance immediately.

2) Proceed as above, giving one breath of artifical ventilation after every five chest compressions.

Controlling bleeding

Heavy blood loss is serious. A reduction in blood pressure leads to shock which can be fatal. Therefore, as soon as breathing is established the next priority is to control bleeding.

1) Apply direct pressure with the fingers to the bleeding points. If the wound area is large, press the sides of the wound firmly but gently together.

2) Raise the injured part and support it in position unless an underlying fracture is suspected.

3) If there are any foreign bodies in the wound do not try to remove them as further damage to veins or arteries may be caused.

Figure 8. Emergency action – a summary

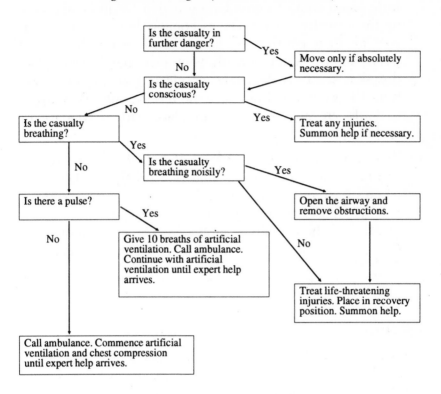

The ABC of resuscitation

A – *Airway:* Tilt the casualty's head and lift the chin to open the airway.

B – *Breathing:* You can oxygenate the casualty's blood by blowing your own expired air into his or her lungs.

C – *Circulation:* Oxygenated blood must circulate around the body, in particular to the brain. If the casualty's heart has stopped, 'chest compressions' can be administered to pump the blood.

4) When you have a dressing available apply it over the wound and press it down gently but firmly. Cover with a pad of soft material. This is then held in position with a bandage. The dressing and pad should extend well above and below the edges of the wound.

5) If the bleeding is not serious, try to reassure the casualty. A little blood seems to go a long way which can be alarming to the casualty. Get them as comfortable as you can. If you are in a position to do so, gently wash the wound with running water. (Wash your own hands first). Dry the skin with sterile swabs or clean tissue. Swab away from the wound and use each swab once only, then apply a sterile dressing pad, held in place with a bandage or sticking plaster.

6) A most important point to remember is that of the risk of tetanus. This is a dangerous infection which can develop if tetanus bacteria enter a wound. Anyone working with or handling horses must be vaccinated. If there is any doubt as to whether the casualty is protected, he or she must go to the doctor or hospital for a quick-acting tetanus injection.

Fractures

A fracture is a broken or cracked bone, caused by a direct force from a kick or blow, or an indirect force, for example a fractured collarbone resulting from falling on an outstretched hand. The two main types of fracture are:

Closed. Where the skin surface is not broken.

Open. Where there is a wound leading to the fracture or when the fractured ends protrude through the skin.

Children's bones are softer than adults, so may not break completely. Such injuries are known as greenstick fractures.

Signs and symptoms of fractures

Pain at or near the site, made worse by movement.

Tenderness to gentle pressure over the affected part.

Loss of control: the casualty cannot move the injured part normally. .

Deformity. This may appear as an irregularity in the bone, a shortening of the limb, angulation or rotation of a limb or as a depression in a flat bone, such as the skull.

Swelling may prevent the recognition of other signs, so when in doubt, treat as a fracture.

The snap of the bone may have been felt or heard.

General rules for treatment

1) Always deal with the ABCs first. Stem any serious bleeding. Ensure that an ambulance has been called for.

2) Unless there is the risk of further injury, treat the casualty on site.

3) The injured part will need to be steadied and immobilized as gently as is possible: immobilize using bandages or an item of clothing.

4) Never offer anything to eat or drink, as the casualty may need an anaesthetic once in hospital.

5) Keep casualty comfortably warm and be reassuring.

Dealing with specific fractures

The collarbone (clavicle)
Likely cause is falling onto an outstretched hand.

Symptoms:

1) Pain, tenderness.

2) The arm on the injured side is partly helpless.

3) The casualty supports the elbow with the head inclined towards the injured side.

Figure 9. Treatment for a collarbone injury

a) The arm on the injured side is first placed in an elevation sling...

b) ... then steadied against the body with a broad-fold bandage.

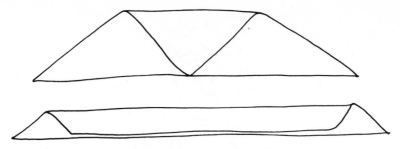

c) How to fold a broad-fold bandage.

Treatment:

1) Sit the casualty down and place the fingers of the hand on the affected side on the opposite shoulder.

2) Place padding between the arm and the body.

3) Using a triangular bandage, place the arm in an elevation sling.

4) Secure the arm to the chest using a broad-fold bandage over the sling.

5) Arrange for transportation to hospital.

The arm

Fractures of the upper arm may occur anywhere along the humerus and be near or involve the elbow joint. Those of the forearm may involve either the radius and/or ulna and also the elbow joint. Fractures should be dealt with as follows:

If the elbow is not involved:

1) Sit the casualty down and place the forearm across the chest, in a position that is most comfortable.

2) Place adequate soft padding between the limb and the chest.

3) Support the limb in an arm sling and secure the limb to the chest using a broad-fold bandage over the sling.

Figure 10. Treatment of broken arm if the elbow is not involved

If the elbow cannot be flexed:

1) Never try to straighten or bend the elbow forcibly.

2) Lay the casualty down.

3) Place the limb gently by the casualty's side, arm to thigh.

4) Place plenty of soft padding between the limb and the body.

5) Secure by three broad bandages tied on the uninjured side of the body:
   (i)   Round upper arm and trunk.
   (ii) Round forearm and trunk.
   (iii) Round the wrist and thighs.

6) Call an ambulance. Check the pulse at the wrist every ten minutes.

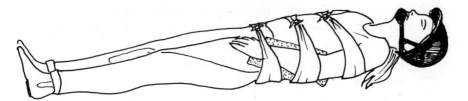

Figure 11. Treatment of broken arm if the elbow is involved

The leg

The thigh bone (femur) may be broken anywhere along its length and must always be regarded as a serious injury due to the great shock accompanied by loss of blood into the surrounding tissues. Often the tibia and fibula are both broken and may well be open. This is common among riders who are kicked by another horse. If the casualty is not already lying down, help them to do so, then treat as follows:

1) Steady and support the injured limb.

2) Bring the sound limb gently to the side of the injured one. Call an ambulance. If the ambulance is to arrive very soon, support the leg with your hands.

3) If you have to move the injured limb, apply very gentle traction and maintain steady support. When moving an injured limb always exercise extreme caution to prevent further damage.

4) If the ambulance is likely to be delayed, you must splint the injured leg to the sound one. Place padding between the thighs, knees, ankles and calves.

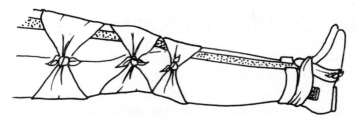

Figure 12. Treatment for a broken leg

5) Secure by tying together with broad bandages:
    (i)   At the ankles and feet with a figure-of-eight bandage.
    (ii) The knees.
    (iii) Above and below the fracture.
    Bandage firmly, but avoid jerky movements.

THE INJURED HORSE

If a horse has been injured in an accident it is very important that you remain as calm as possible — try not to panic.

If the horse looks as though he has suffered a broken leg or similar injury, your main priority is to keep him as still as possible to prevent further damage. Keep him warm by placing jackets or blankets over his hindquarters.

Someone must call the vet immediately. Unfortunately in some cases where a leg is badly broken, the horse has to be humanely destroyed. This is obviously extremely upsetting for everyone, but for the horse's sake try to be calm, soothing and reassuring.

If the horse is injured and unable to get up, the same principles apply — keep him warm, stem any obvious bleeding using clothes or material as padding. Try to keep him as calm and quiet as possible. It is sometimes possible to restrain the horse from struggling by sitting on his neck, near his head. Obviously you must not take dangerous risks.

If the horse is not too badly injured, you must deal with any bleeding on site and arrange transport to get the horse home, again trying to keep him as warm as possible. Once home, call the vet to check thoroughly for any internal injuries.

THE ACCIDENT REPORT

In a licensed school, any accident, however minor, must be reported and written in the accident book. It is a very good idea for everyone, whether at a licensed riding school or private yard, to note down all the relevant details as soon as possible while they are still clear in the mind. This is a great help when insurance claims are being dealt with, as memory can be far from accurate.

From the insurance point of view there is one golden rule to remember after any accident, however caused: never apologize, accept blame or admit liability. Do everything to help where needed. You will need to exchange names and addresses with the parties involved, and note details of their insurance company. Also, collect names and addresses of any witnesses. Once the police arrive on the scene they take over the collection of everybody's details.

The accident report book

When recording details state:

1) Date, place and time of accident.

2) Names, telephone numbers, addresses of everyone concerned, including witnesses.

3) Nature of accident.

4) Probable causes.

5) Injuries received.

6) Treatment given.

7) Whether the emergency services were needed or not.

8) Whether the casualty required hospital treatment.

Also note down anything else you can think of. The report must be signed by the instructor/adult in charge and any witnesses.

As previously mentioned it is highly recommended that anyone working with horses should attend a recognized First Aid course as organized by the Red Cross and St John Ambulance. Hopefully, having taken all the necessary precautions and used lots of common sense, you should enjoy many happy years of safe riding!

6

STAFF MANAGEMENT

Every member of staff plays an important role within the yard team. This team should be structured in such a way that there are clear levels of command. For example, a team may be comprised of:

Owner
Yard Manager   } may be the same person
Head girl/lad
Assistant Instructors
Trainees

All assistants and trainees must know to whom they are answerable and who to consult regarding yard policy. The relationship between the yard manager and the staff will be reflected in the day-to-day organization of the yard.

SKILLS OF THE YARD MANAGER

There is a need for the daily organization to strike a balance between a rigid, inflexible routine which does not allow for those extra, unplanned occurrences and that of an unstructured, chaotic shambles where nothing is planned anyway so any extra 'activities' simply add to the general disarray. This balance is achieved through the many skills of a good yard manager. The implementation of these skills is illustrated in Table 8 below.

Table 8. Management Skills

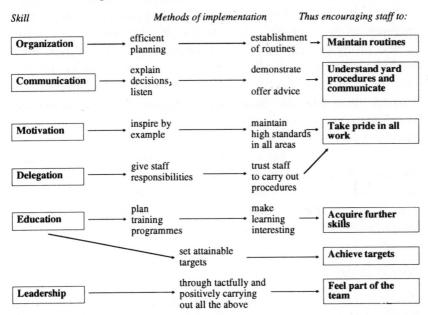

The end result will hopefully be that of a happy working atmosphere with an emphasis on efficiency and quality which may be enjoyed by both staff and horses alike.

Organization of the yard, and establishing yard routines, are dealt with in some detail a little further on. The implementation of other management skills is discussed below.

Communication

The yard manager must communicate with both the staff and any superior, who may be the owner of the establishment. It can be confusing for staff if the owner gives one set of instructions which are then contradicted by the yard manager — this is where good communication plays an important role. The owner should have the confidence to allow the manager to run the yard knowing that he or she will be kept fully updated and informed.

Through liaison with staff on the yard, the manager can experience at first hand how things are running. This makes it easier to detect any potential difficulties and deal with them before they turn into major problems.

Staff should be kept informed of happenings within the business as appropriate, through the development of a system which promotes the free flow of information. This system may include information displayed on notice boards; planning boards may be used to good effect. Brief meetings could be organized, perhaps on a Monday morning, to discuss the programme for the forthcoming week and any problems which may have occurred in the previous one.

Staff should be encouraged to put forward any ideas and discuss matters which may be causing dissatisfaction. A happier atmosphere is created through staff feeling that they are 'in the know'. Team spirit is enhanced and the feeling of 'them and us' is greatly reduced.

Motivation

There is a high turnover of staff within the equestrian industry, which generally occurs as a result of long hours for meagre rewards.

Individual employees should be encouraged to have an ongoing interest in their work — boredom and frustration inevitably lead to a search for employment elsewhere. Staff who feel involved in the running of a yard are more likely to contribute ideas. They will then feel motivated if they can see the effects of their personal efforts, and this will further encourage the use of initiative.

In order to keep staff morale high, certain criteria need to be met, based upon the three Rs:

Respect. All staff/trainees deserve the respect of their superiors.

Recognition. A job well done deserves praise. Praise must be expressed as appropriate — all too often it is only criticism which flows freely. This can have a damaging effect on morale. Any criticism necessary must be constructive and tactfully administered.

Responsibility. Once an employee has learnt how to carry out various tasks to the required level it will boost self-confidence if he or she is trusted with a degree of responsibility.

A friendly working atmosphere helps to keep everyone motivated — it is surprising how one disgruntled member of staff can generate ill-feeling amongst the rest of team.

Delegation

Delegation is an important aspect to consider when reviewing the levels of command within the workforce. All members of staff should understand clearly the yard routine and the nature of the tasks to be performed. Trainees must be taught how to carry out these tasks properly before they are expected to take any degree of responsibility.

The workload must be distributed as appropriate between the workforce to ensure that all tasks are carried out in the most effective manner. The task allocated should match the position of the member of staff, for example it would not be cost-effective to expect the chief instructor to clean tack. His or her skills would be far better utilized in generating income through teaching.

Once tasks have been delegated, staff should be allowed to complete them without constant interference from their superiors. This is not to say that some form of supervision may not be needed, and it must always be understood that, if a difficulty arises, employees have someone to whom they can refer.

Employees will learn through adequate training that all tasks are to be carried out fully to a satisfactory conclusion and not left half-completed.

Methods of performing different tasks may vary from person to person. Provided that the correct end result is achieved with all due regard to safety and efficiency, staff should not be discouraged by having their methods corrected unnecessarily.

The art of delegation lies very much in the ability of the yard manager to distribute the workload without causing the members of staff to feel 'put upon' — this often calls for a considerable degree of tact.

Education

Learning may be described as the acquisition of knowledge. Training is the process of learning with a specific purpose in mind. The student is always more motivated when working towards a target such as an examination or competition.

Regular appraisal of staff enables training needs to be monitored. Training leads to improvement in several areas:

Efficiency. The overall efficiency of the student, making him or her a more valuable member of staff.

Fulfilment. The student's desire to learn is satisfied, helping to keep him or her contented in the job.

Interest. Regular training helps to prevent employees/students from becoming stale.

Motivation. Students are encouraged to try to attain higher levels of achievement.

With time, many organizations become somewhat set in their ways. The accepted way of doing things is often seen as the 'only' way. Training outside the establishment can open up new channels of thought and introduce ideas which might otherwise not be considered. Students may, therefore, benefit through some form of 'off-the-job' training, perhaps spending time at a different yard, in order to experience different ways of doing things.

To ensure thorough preparation for a specific examination or competition, some form of training programme should be prepared. The nature of the training programme will be dependent upon several factors:

1) The duration of the course/time that the student is to be at the centre.

2) Current standard of the student.

3) Age and physical/mental capabilities of student.

4) Student's ambitions and self-motivation.

5) Student's enthusiasm and dedication.

6) Skill of the trainer to motivate and teach.

7) Facilities available at the centre.

The environment should be 'learning' orientated, that is geared towards the training needs of students through the provision of adequate facilities and a well prepared training programme.

Student training may be broadly divided into categories dependent upon the type of yard. These are: riding; stable management; instructing. External training (work in another yard for a specific purpose) may also be appropriate.

Riding
Lessons may be given either in a group (most usual) or privately. Lunge lessons are extremely valuable, and taking part in competitions is an excellent way of gaining experience.

Stable management
Lectures and demonstrations given by the chief instructor or head girl/lad are the usual method of teaching stable management. It may be possible to organize a talk by a local expert, such as a vet, farrier or equine nutritionist to add interest. Lectures should be kept relatively short and students encouraged to listen actively rather than just 'hear'.

It is imperative that all topics covered theoretically are put into practice – it is through actually doing something that the student can truly learn and understand.

A very interesting and low cost method of teaching stable management is by using some of the many videos available. Having watched all or part of a video, a discussion should be held encouraging students to talk about what they have seen.

Students might be asked to produce a project concentrating on one specific aspect of horse care – equestrian magazines have very interesting and up-to-date articles which students should be encouraged to read and possibly use as part of their project.

An in-house library is a great idea — many different books should be kept for the student's use. Other learning material such as magazines, wall charts and leaflets should be available. The videos may be watched in the rest room, keeping the library in which students can study and revise fairly quiet.

Another very good method of learning is through the use of Open Learning (correspondence) courses. Working through a series of test papers ensures that all topics are covered very thoroughly.

Instructing

Students need to watch a skilled instructor giving a lesson and take notes regarding the format and technique. Each student should then prepare several short lesson plans which may be practised using other students as guinea pigs. The same may be done with lecture planning.

External training

There is a great variety of activities and establishments offering the opportunity to gain further knowledge. Visits to different establishments offer stimulation along with an increased awareness of equestrian matters in the outside world. External activities could include visiting the following:

Veterinary centres/research stations.

Different types of yard, such as showing, racing, eventing, polo, driving, showjumping and hunting.

Equestrian museums.

Sales.

To summarize training very briefly, the trainer and trainee must discuss at the onset what is to be the target. The course must be looked at as a whole to ensure thorough coverage of all relevant topics.

The trainer must then use all of his or her expertise in both the subject and management of people to teach the appropriate skills, and also ask the questions:

'Is there an alternative means of teaching this or is the customary, accepted approach the best?' 'Are the students to gain only a superficial knowledge, or should the aim be to acquire a deep level of understanding?'.

Teaching can be made so interesting — students must *understand* PICTA!

Principles
Ideas
Concepts   } must be understood
Theories
Approaches

It is not enough to know how — one must understand 'why'.

ORGANIZATION OF THE YARD

There are many factors which affect the way in which a yard is organized. They include:

1) The number of horses kept.

2) The purpose for which they are kept.

3) The method of keeping the horses, for example whether they are grass kept or stabled.

4) The staff/horse ratio.

5) The experience and quality of the staff.

6) And, last but not least .... the organizational ability of the yard manager!

Horses are labour-intensive, having an almost endless list of associated jobs which need to be attended to on a regular basis. These may go undone or be carried out improperly if planning is inadequate. Whatever the size or nature of a yard it can only benefit from a well thought out routine.

Yard duties

Daily duties tend to be the same in every type of yard:

Checking all horses for general well-being.
Feeding.
Watering.
Filling and soaking haynets.
Mucking out.
Sweeping.
Tidying muck heap.

Turning out/bringing in.
Grooming.
Tacking up and untacking.
Exercising.
Cleaning tack.

Additional matters will need attending to as necessary and include the following:

In the tack room

Clearing shelves and cupboards, cleaning and refilling. Discarding old medicines and very worn items of equipment.

Sorting out, cleaning and mending rugs, numnahs and other items of equine clothing.

Attending to minor repairs.

Cleaning all spare tack and headcollars.

Cleaning and disinfecting grooming kit. Discarding very old, worn brushes.

In the barns and feed rooms

Cleaning and sweeping thoroughly.

Putting down poison for rodents in a safe position (well hidden out of the reach of cats, dogs and horses).

Checking stocks of hay, straw, shavings and feed and ordering as necessary.

Bringing oldest hay forward to ensure it is used before new.

Scrubbing out feed/water buckets.

In the yard

Cleaning out and unblocking drains.

Cleaning and repairing guttering.

Attending to roofing and wiring repairs.

Checking all fire-fighting equipment.

Attending to flower beds, hanging baskets; mowing grassed areas.

In the stables

Hosing and disinfecting.

Cleaning and changing light bulbs.

Removing cobwebs.

Cleaning windows.

Attending to paintwork/creosote.

In the arenas

Harrowing/raking surfaces.

Painting and repairing showjumps.

Keeping gallery area tidy.

In the paddocks

Repairing and maintaining fences, gates and hedges.

Topping, harrowing and fertilizing.

Removing droppings and poisonous weeds.

Repairing field shelter and hay racks.

Removing rubbish, filling in pot holes, removing low branches.

Attending to poached areas.

Scrubbing out troughs and checking lagging on pipes.

Vehicles

Cleaning inside and out.

Maintenance checks including oil, water and tyre pressures.

Checking trailers for maintenance requirements.

Table 9. Sample Routine for a Large Equestrian Centre

Yard staff consists of:
Chief Instructor.   Two Assistant Instructors.
Head girl (Intermediate Instructor).   Several   trainee   working   pupils
                                          (WPs).

All staff live on site.

7.30 a.m.	Head girl checks all horses and feeds assisted by WPs. Horses brought in from fields and fed. Haynets refilled, more hay soaked in fresh water.
7.45	Muck out, set fair, sweep yard, tidy muck heap.
8.45	Breakfast.
9.15	Quarter and tack up horses for first lesson.
9.45	LESSON. Livery horses exercised.
10.45	Exercised horses strapped and all others quartered.
11.15	Coffee break.
11.30	LESSON — WPs' ride.
12.30 p.m.	Strap second lot of exercised horses. Skip out, set fair, sweep, hay and feed.
1.00	Lunch.
2.00	LESSON.
2.15	WPs' stable management talk with head girl.
3.00	LESSON. WPs attend to yard duties as set out on work list.
3.30	Tea break.
3.45	Some WPs teaching practise whilst others clean tack.
4.15	LESSON.
4.30	Skip out, set fair, sweep, fill haynets, soak more hay.
5.30	Evening staff arrive. Everyone else leaves. Horses finished for the day are brushed over and rugged up.
5.30	LESSON.
6.00	Skip out, sweep, hay and water.
6.15	Feed. Leave hay and feeds ready for horses in evening lessons.
6.45	FINAL LESSON. Set fair all stables and hang up haynets.
7.45	Brush down and rug up. Feed. Final check.

Planning aids

A well thought out selection of display planners will help in the general organization of a yard. Each yard will need to design the boards to suit individual requirements. Ideas include:

Year Planner. This needs to be displayed in a communal area such as the rest room. Information shown can include holidays and days off, competition dates and seasonal jobs. A colour coding system can be used for extra clarification.

Month Planner. This board should be positioned near the telephone in the office and can easily be made with a large sheet of white card and clear perspex. The card is marked out with five weeks, each week then divided into seven days. The card is then attached to the wall and covered with the large clear perspex sheet.

The date is written on the beginning of each week with a water-based pen. All bookings/events can be displayed on the board as well as being written down in the office diary. At the end of each month the board can be wiped clean ready for the next month's fixtures.

Daily Work/Ride List. This is prepared the evening before and pinned up on the yard first thing in the morning. Information shown may include:

Times of lectures/lessons.

Names of horses and riders.

Type of exercise each horse requires.

Specific tasks to be completed; clipping, farrier's visits etc.

Feed Room List. The information displayed on this board should include:

The amounts and types of feed given to individual horses.

Any supplements, additives or medications to be mixed in with the feeds.

The amount of hay to give and whether the hay is soaked or not.

Health Checks List. This board should show the twelve months of the year and all horses' names. Information displayed should include:

Date of worming, brand name and amount given.

Date and details of shoeing.

Date of teeth rasping.

Date and details of inoculations.

Any ailments, visits by the vet, treatment and medications.

Stable Boards. In larger yards, small blackboards attached to the inside of every top door are very useful. The board needs to be positioned so that the horse cannot reach it and lick or wipe off the vital information that is displayed. This information can include anything relevant to that particular horse which the yard staff need to know. All boards/lists need to be updated regularly in order to be of value. When used properly they can greatly improve the efficiency of any yard.

Yard Record Books. These books need to be kept by the yard manager. Separate books may be needed to store information about the horses, feed stocks, tack, farrier's and vet's visits.

Horse Records. A filing cabinet containing separate wallets for each horse is the most useful method of storing information. All wallets are filed in alphabetical order and may contain the following:

Name, address and telephone number of owner.

A copy of the livery agreement.

Details of the equipment/tack that arrived with the horse.

Vaccination certificates or passports.

Breeding papers.

Registration papers.

Freeze-marking documents.

Stud records if applicable.

Feed Book. Information stored should include that which is valuable when re-ordering:

Details of each weekly food order and delivery.

Current costs of different feedstuffs.

Current hay/straw/shavings stocks.

Details of feed additives and supplements.

Tack Book. Information stored should include:

An inventory of all tack and equipment belonging to the establishment. This is useful should an insurance claim have to be made, for example after a break-in.

Details of all tack belonging to livery owners.

Details of all tack repairs.

Farriery and Veterinary Book. Information stored should include dates and details of all farrier visits, and of all horse ailments, vet visits, treatment and medication.

This book helps when invoicing livery owners. Often veterinary bills are sent directly to the horse's owner.

Accident Report Book. Any accident on the premises must be recorded in this book, as discussed earlier.

Organization of the office

Whether the office is a small shed adjoining the tack room or a large, specially designated room in the main house, it must be tidy, clean, efficient and well run.

In a busy yard it would be more practical to have a reception area separate from the office, in which clients could pay for their lessons and make their next appointment. This would save on a lot of traffic passing through the office.

Both the reception area and office should be well signposted so the visitor is in no doubt as to where to go.

The reception area

Provide a doormat so people can clean the worst of the dirt from their boots before entering. The flooring material needs to be hard-wearing and easy to clean.

The reception area should create a good first impression — it certainly does not need to be lavishly furnished but should provide a degree of comfort. Seating should be provided and some form of heating will be needed in the winter months. Other furniture needed in the reception area would include a large desk or counter, shelving, a wastepaper bin and a secure cash box or till.

This is the ideal area in which to display the notice board showing details of any activities, lists of fees and yard rules. A payphone may be installed for the use of clients and working pupils. Tea- and coffee-making equipment would add to the sense of welcome.

The office

Furniture needed in the office includes a large desk, sufficient shelving and storage areas such as filing cabinets or chests of drawers. A telephone and answering machine are essential. Other equipment which may be needed includes a typewriter and photocopier.

All yard records should be kept in the office. All paperwork must be kept neatly filed in ring binders or document wallets and stored safely.

Each individual business has its own way of running the office. With a little planning it is not difficult to maintain a good level of office organization.

PUBLIC RELATIONS

It is always desirable for equestrian businesses to strike up a friendly relationship with the public.

Dealing with neighbours

Many horse-related establishments find themselves subjected to hostilities from neighbours who can make life difficult to varying degrees. There are several ways to minimize this:

1) Keep them informed — for example, if you intend to submit a planning application it is often appreciated if you either write to or visit neighbours first and let them know. Any queries can be discussed in the early stages and this may allay any fears and prevent objections from being lodged.

2) Respect their privacy; if your manège borders with their garden, fence it tastefully so it offers them privacy as well as being pleasing to the eye. Neighbours are also entitled to reasonable peace and quiet so try to keep noise to a minimum, particularly early in the mornings at weekends.

3) Respect their property; ensure that riders do not allow the horses onto neighbours' verges when out hacking. Provide sufficient parking space so clients do not have to park their cars in view of or in front of neighbours' houses.

Public relations exercises

Any publicity (provided it is good publicity!) will benefit the business, so prepare some editorial information for inclusion in magazines and newspapers and inform the local press of any newsworthy activities at the establishment and invite a representative down to take photographs and notes.

Prior to opening, a full- or half-page spread may be taken in a local newspaper giving information about the business, services it will offer, etc. To help with the cost of this it is usual to invite suppliers of goods and services to your business to place advertisements within the feature. These normally incorporate some form of 'good luck' message to your new venture.

Open days are useful means of improving the public's awareness of your establishment and the service it provides. These can range from small scale half-day affairs to large all-day ones. Attractions may include displays, demonstrations, equestrian personalities (both equine and human), trade stands etc.

Good public relations greatly improve the business's chances of survival as well as enhancing its image.

Advertising

The nature of your advertising campaign will, to a certain extent, depend upon who and where your customers are. Ideas about where to advertise would include:

Locally: Local press, under leisure activities.
              Tack shop and sports centre.
              Inns, pubs and hotels.
              Restaurants and tea rooms.
              Tourist information centres.
              Radio.
              By jump sponsorship at an event.
              In show schedules.

Nationally: In the BHS publication *Where to Ride*.
              In directories, year books and *Yellow Pages*.
              In magazines — there are many types of publi-
              cations aimed at varying age groups and specialist
              aspects of equestrianism.

Your advertising space will cost the business a large amount of money over the year so advertisements must be clear, informative, eye-catching, and instantly recognizable, for example through the use of a business logo.

An advertising company can design and prepare advertisements so that the proofs may be sent to the magazines, saving on artwork and preparation costs. A careful record must be kept of all advertisements booked, invoiced and paid for.

Work out a system of identifying where the strongest response comes from and which, therefore, is the most cost-effective method of advertising.

CONCLUSION

With the right planning, running your own business can be rewarding, in both personal and financial terms. So, if having read this book you decide to go for it......good luck!

BIBLIOGRAPHY

Bennett, Roger. *Small Business Survival*. Pitman Publishing, 1989.

Houghton-Brown, J. and Powell-Smith, V. *Horse Business Management*. BSP Professional Books, 1990.

Jones, Gary. *Starting Up*. Pitman Publishing, 1990.

West, Alan. *A Business Plan*. Pitman Publishing, 1990.

Whitehead, Geoffrey. *Bookkeeping & Accounting*. Pitman Publishing, 1989.

St. John Ambulance, St. Andrew's Ambulance Association, British Red Cross. *First Aid Manual*. Dorling Kindersley, Sixth Edition, 1992.

INDEX